Southern Living

style

Southern Living style

Easy Updates • Room-by-Room Guide • Inspired Design Ideas

Oxmoor House®

table of contents

ome is where the heart is—a sentiment that is easy to understand when our home reflects who we are and fits our lifestyle like a well-tailored slipcover. After all, the Southern landscape, like the pages of *Southern Living*, is sprinkled with beautiful homes that envelop occupants in style and comfort and invite guests to linger, taking it all in. Yet there is no cookie-cutter formula for achieving great style at home. Many approaches can get you there, but great design is truly in the details. It's the little extras—a thoughtful arrangement of art on the wall, the flourish of a monogram on a pillow, the play of color and texture and light and shadow—that elevate a room's style quotient and make it special.

For many of us, decorating is like entertaining. The consummate host, like the capable decorator, approaches the task with vision, energy, and confidence. There is almost as much pleasure in the process as in the result. A timid entertainer, like a daunted decorator, wrings her hands at the to-do list, frets over the many choices, and often throws her hands up in exasperation at the entire notion and waves a white towel.

If you're easily daunted, fret no more. *Southern Living Style* demystifies the process of creating a beautiful home. Even if you're of a more capable variety, get ready to become even more emboldened.

Inside you'll find beautiful photographs of some of the most inspired interiors from across the South. We highlight the details worth adopting in your own home. Learn from a handful of the region's most notable designers as they walk you through their well-honed approaches to address a variety of design issues. Our staff style makers show you how easy it is to revamp the pieces you already have, proving great design doesn't have to cost a fortune. A coat of paint on an inherited piece or graphic upholstery on an old flea market find can transform it into a one-of-a-kind standout—exactly the sort of unique piece that puts soul into a space…and perhaps heart in your home.

Happy decorating!

Lindsay

Editor, *Southern Living*

defining southern style

defining southern style

hat is Southern style? The nuances can be hard to define, yet when you see a beautiful room like this one, you know all the elements are there: The easygoing mix of formal and informal furnishings. A color scheme that soothes but never bores. Treasured art displayed in a casual way. Window treatments that waver somewhere between frilly and masculine. A pedigreed rug, passed down through generations and now the perfect spot for a lucky dog's naptime. A fine antique chest cozying up to a loosely slipcovered club chair. Taken together, the pieces add up to a graceful look that can only be known as Southern.

Perhaps Alabama-born and now New York-based designer Richard Keith Langham, who collaborated on this very room in Washington, D.C., captures the essence of Southern style best. "Even if I'm working in the most elegant of rooms, I bear in mind creature comforts and livability," he explains. "I'd say it's a Southern thing. I know sweeping generalities are crazy, but I do think Southerners really know how to live."

Contemporary Southern design has transformed in so many ways in recent decades. Along with the rest of the country, Southerners have embraced the simplicities of modern design. Yet, even while so many trends point toward the future, Southerners young and old hold steadfast to the hallmarks of this regional charm. And that contrast is the heart of Southern style.

color *and* pattern

Temperate Southern climates encourage outdoor living year-round, so **colorful interiors, often inspired by nature, have really never gone out of style.** Even in rooms blanketed in neutrals, a pop of color shows up to break the monotony. Though beauty is the motivator, color and pattern can simultaneously serve underlying functions as simple as masking an architectural flaw or the wear and tear of rowdy children armed with crayons. Mixing patterns can be especially effective if a common color unites them. In Atlanta designer Louise Cronan's living room *(below right)*, red walls paired with paisley, striped, and floral prints—all red—do not overwhelm; rather, they create the background for her collections. **Contrasting green curtains virtually go unnoticed,** fading into the foliage outside.

As for designer Fiona Newell Weeks of Easton, Maryland, a damask-patterned wallpaper accented with shimmering chartreuse silk curtains hides her indecision *(left)*. "I could never limit myself to one style," she says, referring also to the floral-patterned pillows thrown into the mix. Her balance of color, pattern, texture, and scale has a welcome note of whimsy, which is a Southern favorite.

take it from *Heidi:*

New Orleans decorator Heidi Friedler suggests letting art inspire your palette. Friedler's inclination toward strong color and graphic prints enjoys free rein in her own living room, where she's been able to take color inspiration from art. **"Artists obviously know how to use color, so I just used the painting as a cue for the palette in the room."** Throughout her house, she follows the lead of her art collection to inspire paint color and fabric choices.

1) **Cheerful floral and striped patterns** of grass green, a color pulled from the painting, with a punch of fuchsia paint and fabric on a formal French chair give this room sophisticated playfulness.

2) **Lacquered apricot walls and a Matelassé-covered sofa** in Palm Beach turn an antiques-filled room into laid-back chic. Orchid-print pillows pop against the white furnishings, and vibrant lime green, plucked from the prints, injects unexpected color. The bergères, originally green, were refinished in white and re-upholstered in a subtle print with contrasting piping to update the look.

3) **Two classic patterns**—toile and gingham—make a bold statement in the library of this 18th-century plantation house on Maryland's Eastern Shore. The upholstered walls are punctuated with turquoise wallpaper inside the bookshelves, inspired by the vibrant glass drops of the chandelier—the happy result of a shopping trip to an Atlanta antiques mall.

slipcovers

Before air-conditioning, Southerners traditionally slip-covered their upholstered pieces in summer when the windows were open in an attempt to cool the house. Slipcovers protected furnishings from dust and dirt that sneaked in with bugs and breezes and could be easily removed and laundered. Mahogany legs and arms were often left exposed for a stylish contrast with the conventional cotton muslin covers, much like Birmingham designer Mary Evelyn McKee's kitchen chairs (*below right*). "Slipcovers are best when they are precisely made and hang clean and close to the body of the piece," she says. **"Think of them like dresses—best when they hug the body, but not too tightly or with too many frills.** They make me think of summer shifts I wore years ago. I often use artist canvas from the art-supply store and bleach it when it gets dirty."

collections

The passion of **collecting—plundering flea markets, road trips to antiques shows, scanning eBay in the wee hours—borders on addiction.** And Southerners collect with abandon, whether it's an obscure silver pattern to set the table or a collection of globes *(below)* dating to the 1800s, sought out to add an air of scholarship to a room. Key West designer Michael Pelky is no exception. **Though an avid collector, he has learned to decorate with restraint. "I must have more than 200 ironstone pudding molds," says Pelky** (cooking was his profession for 15 years). To accommodate such massive numbers *(right)*, he designed a bookshelf in his living room to neatly display the molds. Notice his collection of ironstone pitchers tucked away at the top. (Cool idea: The built-in cabinet at the bottom hides the television.)

take it from *D'Ette:*

Austin, Texas, entrepreneur, artist, and collector D'Ette Cole displays collections, big and small, to inspire happy memories. A longtime fixture on the local antiques scene (formerly a partner in Uncommon Objects, a shop known for anything one of a kind), Cole lives with her collections all around her, from the lighthearted column of Chinese fortunes tacked up at random to the more serious vintage paintings and ironstone pottery. "Everything in my house is eclectic and sentimental and nods to different periods and styles, which, in my mind, is more true to how people really live." Her favorite fortune: "Very little is needed to make a happy life."

1) **Glass-front cabinets** showcase a collection of creamware, a type of earthenware popular from the late 1700s through the early 1800s. Though arranged with little restraint, the cabinet shows off the goods while keeping them neatly contained. The all-white case, paired with its all-white wares, makes for a dramatic, monochromatic effect.

2) **Unusual twists** are designer D'Ette Cole's signature, like using an old post office mail sorter (rather than a traditional bookcase) to hold her design books. "I like to present things in vignettes that change the way you would normally see them."

3) **Collections** aren't always meant to simply sit on the shelf. This set of Mottahedeh's Blue Canton china sets the table for lively dinner parties when it's not decorating the shelf.

4) **History and tradition** should be toasted. Nothing's more Southern than a mint julep—crushed ice, bourbon, sugar, and a sprig of fresh mint. Families collect julep cups and pass them down through the generations. Anything inscribed on them—the date of a memorable event or a monogram—makes them all the more coveted.

monograms

A Southern tradition borrowed from Europeans, who adapted the custom from aristocracy, monograms were first used to mark personal items, like jewelry and linens. Before a lady married, she would monogram items in her trousseau with her maiden initials. After she married, it was correct to add the letter of her married name, accompanied by either her first and maiden names or first and middle initials, hence the modern-day monogram. In recent years, Southerners have taken the idea a bit further: "We monogram everything from tote bags to planes," says Palm Beach decorator Leta Austin Foster. White-on-white is the most traditional combination for linens, but royalty often chose red—and commoners followed suit, adding decorative laurels and bows.

"Ivory hemstitch napkins with a gold monogram are the little black dress of tabletop," says Jane Scott Hodges, founder of the couture linen company Leontine Linens. She also likes a more contemporary approach of a single large initial, like the one used by Atlanta designer Betty Burgess (*right*). "Being from the South, of course I love a monogram. But I wanted to put a spin on tradition, so I had it painted," says Burgess.

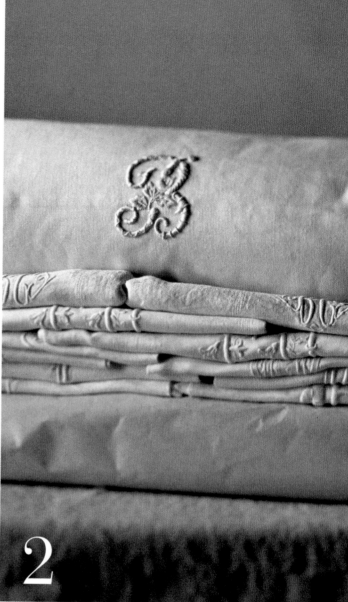

1) **The embroidered numbers** of the dining chairs are a clever twist on traditional monogrammed style. Frequent guests of Style Director Heather Chadduck get a "number" in lieu of a place card. "I have a signature font that appears in every room," she says.

2) **Antique linens** have grown in popularity as collectors' items, in particular dinner napkins and accent pillows like these. No need to worry if the initials match your own—use them anyway.

3) **Monogrammed 1930s Baccarat glasses** inherited from her husband's great-grandmother grace the table of hostess Debbie Winsor of Washington, D.C.

4) **A fanciful pale-green monogram** repeated on the pillows and coverlet adds just a touch of color to an otherwise all-white bed. The monogram design is by Jane Scott Hodges of Leontine Linens.

take it from *Jane Scott:*

Jane Scott Hodges, founder of Leontine Linens of Atlanta, New Orleans, and Lexington, Kentucky, says to toss prudish etiquette aside when using monogrammed pieces. **"Traditionally, a woman would use her first, maiden, and married initials,"** says Hodges, **"but I encourage clients to use whatever makes them happy."** Most men put initials inside their tuxedo coat or on barware, not linens. "Does your husband notice what's on the bed? If he does and it would mean something to him to have his initials on a pillow, then by all means include him," she says with a laugh. And there's nothing wrong with using a found piece either. "Throw it on the table and say it was your Aunt Edith's."

3

4

wicker, rattan
cane, *and* bamboo

Outdoor living not only implies living in the garden, but it also invites bringing the garden inside—with color and humble furnishings typically intended for the outdoors. **Wicker, rattan, cane, and bamboo decorate the finest (as well as more modest) rooms in the South, probably evolving from the tradition of loggias and sunrooms.** Although such pieces are often considered the equivalent of less formal "beach house furniture," they can unpredictably adapt to upscale interiors. "My cottage is in a National Register historic district," says Janet Gregg, a Charleston, South Carolina, designer with a self-professed "chair fetish." Yet she fills it with **quirky pieces, like the painted rattan chair (*left*), elevating its status with a velvet throw pillow.**

Baton Rouge, Louisiana, designer Carl Palasota also fills his house with one-of-a-kind antiques and quirky flea market finds. The wicker hamper, now a sideboard in his dining room (*right*), was once used by an importer to transport artwork.

1) **Vintage bamboo chairs** found at a Paris flea market set the tone of this lakeside dining room in Hot Springs, Arkansas. Designer Kevin Walsh likes them because they don't obstruct the view. "You can see through their backs," he explains.

2) **A wicker chair** is painted red and used as a resting place for Charleston, South Carolina, designer Janet Gregg's art books. "I don't follow decorating rules—I just know what I like," she says. "I use chairs and stools for other purposes like book stands and side tables."

3) **The dining chairs** in Lee Kleinhelter's breakfast nook serve up a twist—they're actually painted vintage fiberglass, not wicker!

4) **Formality and comfort** find a balance in this New Orleans dining room designed by Gerrie Bremermann. Caned-backed Louis XVI armchairs contribute to the dressed-down feeling, while a more dressed-up buffet, chandelier, and trumeau mirror lend to the room's formality.

4

take it from *Lee:*

Lee Kleinhelter, owner of Pieces, Inc., in Atlanta, uses cane, wicker, or rattan pieces. **"I love exaggerated shapes and a Hollywood Regency influence, but natural materials downplay the glamour, making pieces easier to work with in a room.** If I find a piece already painted and in good shape, I'll do nothing more than clean it up. If it needs painting, find a professional. If you don't prep it correctly, you'll find it chipping and flaking once it dries. I always opt for a semigloss—super glossy lacquer will show every imperfection, and matte is just too flat for me."

the hearth

Whether blazing with warmth in the winter or quietly undisturbed in the heat of summer, the fireplace inevitably draws a crowd—likely the gathering place for many a lively family conversation and old-fashioned Southern storytelling. **As the focal point of a room, it can also reveal a lot about a homeowner's style.** In earlier times most kitchens had a fireplace used to prepare meals, like this one (*right*) in Maryland unearthed during a renovation and now used as a nap spot for the owner's dogs. **The more traditional living room fireplace is often decorated with a single mirror or painting flanked by a pair of vases or sconces or a group of objects.** The trick is to weight the arrangement so that it looks and feels balanced.

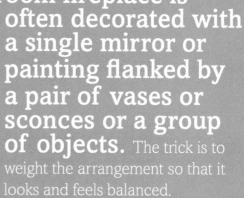

Fort Worth designer Joe Minton's hearth, decorated with a collection of antique Staffordshire dogs, is flanked by built-in bookcases (*left*). "I'm a dog lover," he explains. Notice the dog portrait that tops off his look.

painted floors

Painted wood floors have become so fashionable in Southern interiors that it comes as quite a surprise their next of kin is the widely out-of-favor linoleum. **The popularity of painting floors likely grew from early European painted floorcloths—hence, linoleum's evolution—that were used to cover and decorate inferior-cut wood floors** (better wood cuts were limited to the most formal rooms). Later, in the 1800s, wood floors were elevated with paint to simulate stone. "I've always been drawn to geometric patterns," says Baton Rouge designer Carl Palasota, referring to the overscale diamond pattern on his living room floor (*left*). "I painted them freehand with sponge brushes for an irregular look." **The rustic simplicity of alternating squares of natural wood has a sophisticated, surprisingly modern look.** A simpler approach, used in a Virginia bedroom (*right*), is a solid wash of color that gets better with the scuffs and scratches of age.

luxe curtains

The South has come a long way since Miss Scarlett wore hers, but **bountiful curtains still decorate every room of the house.** Well-appointed windows are both functional and flattering. **While controlling light, privacy, warmth, and sound, draperies provide a finishing touch to a room in the form of color, pattern, texture, and shape.** Curtains allow for many interpretations of style, like the use of dressmaker details—fringe, tassels, and tiebacks—that create an embellished look. The way they hang from the ceiling also contributes to the overall vibe of the room. In Palm Beach, Florida, Lars Bolander lets silk fabric puddle indulgently, glamorously on the floor (*left*)—a more tailored approach would let them barely kiss the floor at the bottom. An over-the-top use of pale-blue toile (*right*) in a third-floor bedroom, tucked under the slanting roofline of this house, creates a cocooning canopy of draperies.

Using a unifying fabric with curtains can turn odd architecture into a cool framework.

take it from *Gerrie:*

Gerrie Bremermann, a New Orleans designer, embraces simple textures and tailored treatments for stylish curtains. "I'm a purist. I love 100 percent silk, 100 percent cotton, and 100 percent linen. I think you can do an elegant house in cotton. I love simple, loosely pleated curtains on iron rods and rings."

1) **A box-pleated valance** above the curtain panels hides the rod and keeps light from seeping in at the top.

2) **Sheer undercurtains** hang on a separate rod behind the main curtains. They can be pulled for a dappled light when the solid, lined curtains remain open.

3) Tiebacks—a band of fabric, cording, or trim used to pull the curtain back from the window—are typically used in formal, traditional settings. They look best in older homes with pretty windows that need to be shown off. These tiebacks are placed unusually low to let in more light.

4) Elaborate trims look best on simple, solid-colored panels. Interesting hardware can make up for lack of architectural detail.

> **"I am always looking at fashion for interesting details,"** says Atlanta designer Jackye Lanham. "The finishes on a curtain are like the details on a well-made dress—colored or patterned lining, a grosgrain trim, a ruffle, or a frayed edge make curtains beautiful."

portraits

Portraits are prized treasures for their representation of the very likeness of a person, down to facial expressions and even mood. Today, however, especially among younger collectors all over the country, there is a trend toward more modern, contemporary art with an evolving array of subjects from landscapes to abstracts. **Even so, Southerners have not completely abandoned their penchant for the past, which has long included portraits of ancestors passed down through the generations. In fact, mixing these old favorites with modern pieces has actually created more eclectic interiors.** For instance, ancestral portraits are displayed in a most unexpected place—just above bowls of fruit and stacks of coffee mugs in the kitchen (*left*). Some portraits are not inherited, but collected.

Atlanta designer Jackye Lanham pulled the color scheme (*right*) for her clients' dining room from their collection of antique portraits purchased here and there.

antiques

Southerners can't claim the obsession with antiquing as theirs alone, but their motivations are unique. Antiques dealer Sumpter Priddy of Alexandria, Virginia, considers the difference: "In the North, it's all about the academic subtleties. In the South, it's more about where it came from and who owned it." **Most importantly, aside from provenance, his advice is: "I look for a piece that truly grabs me."** Priddy shops with the heart, much like New Orleans designer Gerrie Bremermann, who claims that, in a perfect world, "every time my heart stopped over a chair or commode, I would buy it— you never need to change the things you love." Though many Southerners incorporate only inherited antiques into their decor, others travel to antiques shows or visit specialty shops. Birmingham designer Mary Evelyn McKee bought this French empire sofa (*left*) from a dealer in Atlanta who bought it off the back of a truck in Paris. The growth of Internet antiques sites has further increased options. Still others go about it the old-fashioned way—by word of mouth. Atlanta designer Louise Cronan found her painted Regency-style center table (*right*) through her hairdresser, who spotted it in Las Vegas.

1) **Antique textiles** can be used to throw over tables or the back of the sofa for a pop of color, but here an antique Indian bed hanging, or palampore, is loosely suspended from the ceiling for an elegant twist on the traditional headboard.

2) **Antiques** can be functional as well as pretty. Style Director Heather Chadduck won her antique Chambers stove on eBay. "I actually bought two—same model, same year—and melded the best of both." Chambers gas stoves, which became popular after World War I, can take anywhere from 40 to 200 hours of painstaking restoration, depending on the condition.

3) **A traditional English-style antique buffet** gets a youthful update painted green and paired with contemporary art and graphic, modern lamps.

3

take it from *Sumpter:*

Alexandria, Virginia, antiques dealer and scholar Sumpter Priddy urges his clients to arm themselves with information before they buy. "Ask a lot of questions: Can the dealer show you other pieces you can compare it to? Does it have provenance? If not, is this reflected in the price? Consider your motivations: Are you shopping for something that will make you smile on a rainy day, or do you have a need to fill? We all look for pieces that satisfy both, but it's important to know what your goal is. If you are specifically looking for a sideboard, come armed with research, but don't discount the unexpected treasure that finds you."

living southern in every room

living southern *in* every room

s we move through the Southern home and pay attention to the multiple uses and styles of each room, we realize that every space is equipped with the comforts of everyday living as well as the beautiful furnishings and accoutrements required for entertaining. In thoughtfully and carefully designed rooms, functional practicality and formality mingle harmoniously.

Southerners have a penchant for the past and often live in older homes, where they frequently squeeze modern conveniences into antiquated spaces. This can lead to the quirky beauty that is indicative of the region's decorating style. There are the hardworking rooms, like bathrooms outfitted with the newest hardware and tile, techno-savvy home offices equipped with the most up-to-date gadgets, and an occasional kitchen featuring the addition of a modern industrial range. And then there are the rooms where the "living" takes place. A successfully decorated living room, though well collected, will not ignore the need for comfortable furnishings. A dining room may inspire lively conversation with colorful design, but the chairs at the table will never be ghastly uncomfortable for guests. As Charleston, South Carolina, designer Amelia Handegan notes, "I like my house to feel warm and welcoming, but I design for life, not for show."

(Left) In Amelia Handegan's Charleston family room, upholstered furnishings are comfortably covered in plush, soft fabrics. The 1960s Volkswagen orange of the coffee table, which she designed, provides a whimsical pop of color among the antiques and nonconventional wall hangings she collected during her travels.

entryways

Often the smallest (and most duplicitous) room of the house, the entryway makes the biggest impression about your home's personality—and yours—while, at the same time, creatively concealing the daily accumulation of keys, mail, and umbrellas.

Grand entrances in the South most likely evolved from the long-ago days of no air-conditioning, when many homes were built in the dogtrot style—an architectural concept designed to capitalize on cooling breezes with a wide, open central passage from the front door to the back door of the house. On hot summer days, both doors were swung open, and families often ate, entertained, relaxed, and even slept in the breezeway. With today's evolving architectural designs—thank goodness for central air—entries come in all shapes and sizes, yet the combination of utility and style working together makes the best presentation at the front door.

(Left) Pops of color drawn from the patterned runner in this casual entryway make a cheerful statement. The generous size of the room allows for seating and a console for displaying a pretty arrangement, propping art, and hiding clutter in the drawer space beneath.

graphic punch

Entryway of decorator Heidi Friedler
New Orleans, Louisiana

Why it works:

Modern shapes. The custom-designed
console table and architectural-shaped lamp
are twists on the traditional tableau (chest,
chair, lamp, and mirror).

Bold color. Used against a neutral background, it often works best with graphic
shapes, such as the simplicity and sleekness
of the console and slipper chair.

Ancestral influences. An antique rug
and a collection of old boxes mix with the
contemporary pieces to give the room a
sophisticated playfulness.

designer cue

When you don't have drawers, use
bowls, baskets, and trays, like this
gold-trimmed one on the console, to
provide a pretty place to drop your
keys and mail.

preppy meets formal

Entryway designed by Janie Molster
Gloucester, Virginia

Why it works:

Gutsy wallpaper. "It was the beginning of a vision and became what we all worked around," says Molster. With a hint of silver leaf, the damask wallpaper adds a touch of formality in keeping with the architectural trims and finishes. The well-edited room works sans mirror or artwork, with the wallpaper taking center stage.

Contrast of styles. Preppy color and casual elements contrast more serious architectural detail. In spite of the elegant light fixtures, a simple Shaker-style bench tones down the grandeur, finding surprising harmony beside an ornately carved planter.

Durability. Spiffed up with stain-resistant linen fabrics, the bench is armed and ready for the wear and tear from the children who live here. An inexpensive sea grass rug (easily replaceable through most any mail-order catalog) anticipates lots of traffic.

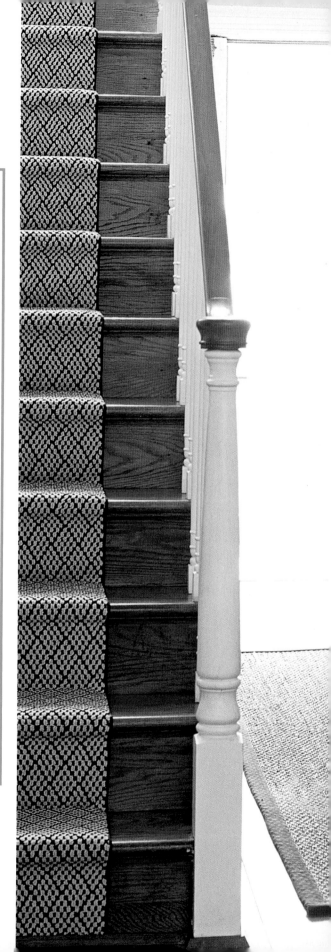

fresh ideas: *accessorizing entryways*

(Organized chaos looks good when everyday items have a designated spot. Here, even the grocery list gets displayed on the chalkboard-painted wall.)

(A lighthearted assortment of this and that looks perfectly composed in this tiny entry space.)

(A picture ledge keeps family photos easily interchangeable and up-to-date.)

(One graphic piece keeps it simple and makes an impressive impact.)

pulling it all together:

start with...

Console table. It works well in a small space, and a pretty bowl or tray atop can neatly accommodate clutter like keys and mail.

Chest. A good choice for large spaces, a chest is perfect for hiding those important things you need as you run out the door—camera, iPod, even a laptop.

Settee. Aside from giving your house a cozy, comfortable welcome, it's a nifty perch for tying your running shoes or just plopping your purse.

top with...

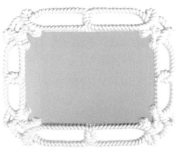

Mirror. Simple or ornate? Let the style of your house decide.

Art. One strong piece or a collection of smaller pieces will do the trick. And, of course, include fresh flowers if you're expecting guests.

add...

Lamp. Or include a pair of them, depending on the space. If there's minimal or no surface area, go with sconces on the wall. When considering a hanging fixture, double check your ceiling height— 7 feet from the bottom of the fixture to the floor is plenty of clearing for the tallest of guests.

throw out the welcome mat...

Rug. Going rug-less is an option, especially in a really small entryway, but in a high-traffic area rugs protect the floor underneath.

Runner. This type of rug is typical since entries often tend to be long and narrow, though if you have an antique rug you want to use, don't opt out because the size isn't perfect. Consider a custom sea grass cut to fit the space and throw the older rug on top. An animal skin is a nice surprise for modern interiors.

living rooms

Living rooms have evolved from the prim and proper parlors to casual spaces accommodating the daily routine of modern families. In the Old South, only the finest fabrics and furnishings were used to decorate such rooms, and children were rarely allowed entrance. Today, we see a more relaxed approach, so that the moniker, for many, has become "family room." As Charlottesville, Virginia, shopkeeper and mother-of-two Christy Ford explains, "For now, the formality has left our house. We're just going with where we are in life."

Nonetheless, this is a room that requires decorating attention and thoughtful furnishings. Upholstered pieces are paramount for comfort. End tables and coffee tables hold lamps, drinks, and books. A television must be accommodated, displayed openly or cleverly disguised. Bookshelves must be filled, and a rug underfoot is another big decision. Across the country, the needs of modern families have resulted in a market full of durable, stain-resistant fabrics; more approachable accessories and furnishings; and even more mainstream choices for floor coverings, like sea grasses and other natural fibers.

Although modern layers have entered even the most traditional living and family rooms across the South, folks have managed to keep their treasured heirloom pieces mixed among them. Atlanta designer and avid collector Louise Cronan puts it this way: "I try to be practical, but mostly I do what I want and live with the scarring." That means ignoring the nicks and scratches on her antique tortoise-glazed coffee table. In the South it's called "patina."

This Amelia Handegan-designed living room filled with heirlooms lacks nothing in comfort. The upholstered furnishings—the oversize wing chair, in particular—cut the formality with welcoming coziness.

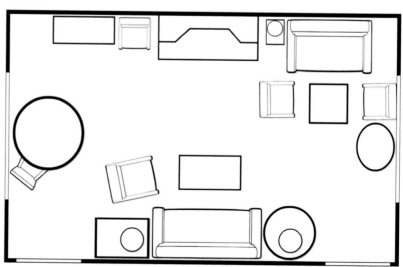

designer cue

The secret to letting kids and animals really live in the house: "Slipcovers—everything is washable," Ford explains. "I purposely choose white because you can bleach it to remove stains."

perfectly practical

layered simplicity

Living room of shopkeeper Christy
Ford, Charlottesville, Virginia

Why it works:

Accessories shine against a neutral background. Charlottesville, Virginia, shopkeeper
and homeowner Christy Ford suggests using a
creamy paint color for a subdued background
that allows the artwork and objects to be the
stars. "I'm kind of obsessed with blue French
opaline glass now," she says. "I would go crazy
with that color, but I learned from my mother to
keep the base neutral in order to let the accessories shine."

Easily interchangeable pieces. This space,
once formal in Ford's pre-children life, has been
dressed down for her growing family's multiple
viewings of *Dora the Explorer*. Ford is a believer
in swapping out furniture to accommodate one's
lifestyle. Her mantra: You can always change it
back. "I tire of things quickly," Ford says. "I've
gone through phases with several different
colors, so I try to change things up with pillows
and throws." The walls and slipcovers stay the
same as she flirts with new color obsessions and
moves furniture around the house. For example,
the previous kitchen table now holds a display of
books and objects.

Multiple seating arrangements. The size of
the room allows for multipurpose use. The sofa,
chair, and coffee table placement accommodates
cozy conversation; the library-dining table can be
cleared on a whim for an impromptu dinner; and
a desk tucked away by the fireplace functions as
a place to return calls or check e-mails.

downtown chic

Living room of designer Lucy Gillis
Athens, Georgia

Why it works:

Freewheeling mix of styles. A modern chrome director's chair looks right at home among traditional furnishings, like an antique spool bench and an old-fashioned settee updated with a graphic, contemporary pattern. An antique rug contrasts with the contemporary striped runner layered over a neutral sisal floor covering.

Confident color. Pops of green, red, and yellow are grounded by notes of black throughout—the settee pattern, the rugs, lampshades, art, and painted chest.

Found objects. Each piece has a sentimental story. The vintage Louis Vuitton trunk and the art school portraits above the settee were found on summer trips to Maine, where Gillis and her sister scour thrift stores and estate sales. "I guess it's easier to buy new stuff, but I enjoy finding special things or decorating with hand-me-downs," she says. The red cocktail table is one thing new—it's a one-of-a-kind piece designed by her aunt.

designer cue

Take a laid-back approach to art in a room that has a carefree vibe. Brass tacks pushed directly into the wall hang unframed portraits above the sofa. For more examples, see page 67.

modern elegance

Living room designed by Carl Palasota
New Orleans, Louisiana

Why it works:

Sense of place. Decorating with the local culture in mind adds personality to the room. Nods to Creole culture, such as a tole chandelier representative of the French influence in the area, and a pair of Audubon prints, reflecting the habitats of local wildlife, quietly define the New Orleans location.

Contrasting shapes. The circular-shaped cocktail table and curvaceous floor lamp soften the angular shapes of the side chair and sofa. "The geometry and classicism of the painted tole chandelier speak to me," says designer Carl Palasota.

Ladylike textures. Natural light filters through closed sheers and bounces off warm, white-lacquered plaster walls. Bouillon fringe and ruffled silk pillows add a feminine touch to the otherwise masculine lines of the sofa.

buttoned-up bohemian

Living room of designer Tyler Colgan, Atlanta, Georgia

Why it works:

Bloomsbury vibe. Patterned textiles—a paisley throw draped over a pedestal table, ikat-printed cushions on a bamboo chair, and an antique rug thrown effortlessly in place over sea grass—add rich color and interest to the room. Academic accents like apothecary-style containers on the coffee table and an old printing spool-turned-lamp by the sofa complete the eclectic look.

Quirky style. Pieces from flea markets, favorite online sources, and even dumpster dives reflect Atlanta designer Tyler Colgan's artsy, spontaneous look. "I filled this house in one day with 20 years of collections," she says. The sofa and chandelier were lucky finds at an antiques mall; both were refurbished. The painting and ready-made curtains are both from mail-order catalogs. She stumbled upon the reading lamp at a church bazaar.

Traditional elements. Classic fabrics, like ticking stripes, checks, linens, and leather, keep the room interesting along with its simple architectural board-and-batten walls and exposed ceiling. Sea grass flooring, a cane coffee table, and a bamboo chair are also timelessly chic.

fresh ideas: *customizing living rooms*

Disguise the Television

(Folding doors enclose or expose the television.)

(By working the television into the vignette of art and books, it seemingly goes unnoticed.)

Stylize the Bookshelves

(Organic meets vintage for graphic appeal.)

(Aside from a few family photos and collectibles, these colorful shelves are loaded with the couple's vast assortment of CDs.)

(A pair of freestanding shelves keeps a uniform tone with antique books.)

Try a Simple Palette

(The patterns are across-the-board, but a mono-chromatic red-and-white scheme holds the look together.)

(Hints of gray and accents of green soften the high-contrast black and white.)

Hang at Random

(Forgoing symmetry, this arrangement of art lends lived-in casualness to a formal room.)

(A grid of pieces on a wall easel is reminiscent of old-fashioned picture molding.)

(Family photos hang in various sizes and styles of black frames.)

sofa *(details)*

(camel back)

(antique settee)

(knole)

(traditional english style)

(tufted)

(sectional)

(modern)

(camel back) Originating in the 18th-century designs of Thomas Chippendale and George Hepplewhite, the feminine lines of this sculptural form become modern with fresh, updated fabrics.

(antique settee) Most likely found in a more formal setting, settees are sought after for cocktail conversation as opposed to relaxation. Most have wooden frames, and this one in particular, in the French Empire style, has sculptural appeal.

(knole) The considerable depth with hinged sides creates a comfortable cocoon. Exposed wooden finials at the rear top corners are tied with a decorative braid or rope. When untied, the sides fold outward to lie flat. These sofas were originally made in the 17th century as a formal throne on which the monarch would sit to receive guests.

(traditional english style) Probably the most popular, these sofas can be found in a variety of lengths in most mail-order catalogs. The most traditional will have three seat cushions, as well as three back cushions.

(tufted) Traditional English-style sofas also come with tufted backs as opposed to cushions for a slightly more formal, tailored look.

(sectional) Sectionals are making a comeback in modern spaces, and they tuck nicely into awkward corners. The style maximizes seating in a room and is known for comfort.

(modern) As many modern designers are creating their own furniture lines for a variety of furniture makers, the market has seen a flood of upholstered furnishings, playing off traditional styles but capitalizing on more graphic, angular shapes.

pulling it all together:

start with...

Sofa. Choose a style that suits your look: traditional (above), sculptural (below, wood framed), or contemporary (bottom, tufted).

Decide on its **placement**—against a long wall, in front of a window, or in the middle of the room—to determine the length needed.

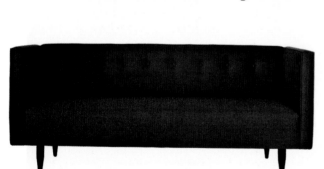

Allow **space** for end tables or floor lamps.

flank with...

End tables and **lamps.** Consider the sofa; don't put a dainty table next to one that is overstuffed and monstrous.

End table **height** should typically hover right around the height of the sofa arm, and the table's surface space helps determine the circumference of lamps.

If the sofa is going to be a place for reading, consider taller lamps. A pair is nice but not necessary as long as one complements the other. Going with **floor lamps** can eliminate end tables if the coffee table is long enough to accommodate both ends of the sofa.

place the...

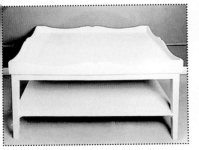

Coffee table. Options include square, round, long, and vertical tables, or even a pair of square tables pushed together for a unique look. Typical height is around 19 inches.

Ottoman. For a put-your-feet-up, laid-back look, an ottoman can also add extra seating in smaller rooms, though it's important to accessorize it with a tray to place drinks or a vase of flowers.

A traditional wooden table accommodates stacks of books and decorative pieces—it's also a great place to serve aperitifs.

add...

Upholstered chairs. Club chairs provide extra comfort, especially if there's room enough for an ottoman.

Occasional chairs. Whether sleek and modern with a splash of chrome or wood framed with an antiqued patina, beautiful chairs often punctuate the style of the room.

Color. Splurge on an expensive fabric, because chairs require less yardage. If a chair is not in close proximity to the coffee table or another surface, it's important to place a cocktail table at its side.

finish off with...

Floor covering. Traditional or modern, consider mixing styles. Rooms with contemporary furnishings often flourish with a rich, traditional rug. Likewise, a modern rug can add flair to a classic room.

If customizing a rug, like natural sea grass, to fit a room, the general rule is to leave 8 to 12 inches of space between the wall and the edge of the rug.

Throwing smaller rugs on top of large ones adds color and defines areas of the room.

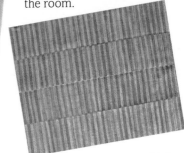

New Orleans decorator Heidi Friedler accents her mostly white kitchen using her mother's collection of aqua Le Creuset cookware from the 1960s. The crystal chandelier adds unexpected glitz to an otherwise classic kitchen with traditional cabinetry, nickel hardware, and glass-front cabinets.

kitchens

The Southern kitchen is perhaps the room that has changed the most over the last 200 years. Once located in an "outbuilding" or other separate structure from the house (due to fire concerns), the kitchen was devoted solely to the endeavor of cooking. Today, it's the hub of activity, even attracting guests during both formal and informal parties. Its status has elevated so that the kitchen has become just as decorated as the rest of the house, with antique furnishings and fixtures, attractive window treatments, and artwork. Not to say the joy of cooking is missing from the modern kitchen; it's just an often more luxurious workspace, especially with the inspired designs of modern appliances. As Atlanta designer and creative director Jill Brinson says, "Life's too short not to have a fabulous kitchen."

Today we see rooms with multiple refrigerators, state-of-the-art gas ranges, and plenty of shelving and cabinetry to accommodate small appliances and other necessities. Of course, there are still those well-loved, dressed-down cottage charmers with the appeal of open shelving, hanging pots, and farm sinks. No matter the style, kitchens have evolved across the board from not only a place to eat but also to do homework, read the paper, and linger over coffee and conversation.

"I always describe this as 'the porch Mama turned into a kitchen when she got electricity,'" says Atlanta architect Jim Strickland.

cottage charmer

Kitchen designed by architect
Jim Strickland, Atlanta, Georgia

Why it works:

Efficient layout. No wasted space and easy movement from stove to sink to island. The island, a straightforward worktable, provides extra counterspace and storage. (It's covered in zinc, like an old-fashioned bar, making it easy to wipe down and keep clean.)

Old-house character. Traditional blue ceilings call to mind an old porch, as do the long windows, which bring light and air over the counters. All the pieces in this kitchen look like furniture moved from other rooms—even the bottom cabinets have legs so they look like a pair of old dressers.

Practical features. Plate racks, instead of wall cabinets, let in natural light. A hanging fixture with metal shades above the island, a single pendant light over the sink, and two metal sconces provide ample task lighting. Instead of a wall of glazed tile, panels of Galvalume® metal roofing protect the wall behind the range from scorches and splatters.

designer cue
On the floor, painters put down an undercoat of black and then painted rosy red on top so hints of black will appear as it ages.

bungalow style

Kitchen designed by Style Director
Heather Chadduck
Birmingham, Alabama

Why it works:

Subtle color contrast. The white and pale gray of the island's marble top (contrasted with stainless steel elsewhere) inspired the palette. The walls, trim, and upper cabinets are bright white; the lower cabinets, windows, and floor stripes are soft gray. The beaded board ceiling got a coat of soft, powder blue.

Architecturally inspired. The upper cabinets have nine panes of glass and are lined with beaded board. The lower cabinets and island facade are inset with the same material.

Form meets function. Serving pieces are displayed in glass-front cabinets to make them easy to find. A center island accommodates a gas cooktop and also provides much-needed storage along with a casual spot for dining. Custom, easy-to-wash linen "hats" top the iron barstools.

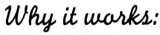

old-world

Why it works:

Rustic finishes. An extra-deep, odd-shaped stone sink with classic two-lever hardware, a wood-beamed 18-foot ceiling, and lightly stained cabinets which hide the modern conveniences give this kitchen a sense of history.

No-fuss arrangement. Aside from a movable island, a single span of counterspace with a maximized depth of 30 inches (typical counter depth is 25 inches) is the only surface space. Nickel-plated, wall-mounted halogen lamps provide task lighting, and custom steel-framed windows emphasize the view of the backyard garden.

Tile invasion. A converted closet in an adjacent room now sets off the stove. The walls and ceiling are covered in old-school, white subway tiles.

parisian flair

Kitchen of homeowners Angie and Blake Cordish
Baltimore, Maryland

Why it works:

Custom made to look old. The homeowner designed the stucco hood, trimmed in stone, to fit a giant antique French butcher-block snugly into place by the stove. Stone laid in a grid pattern of contrasting color covers the floor.

Quirky accents. A ceramic cow's head, from an old French shop, stands guard over the stove. A far wall houses a grid of collected hooks that hold keys, hats, umbrellas, and such. Instead of conventional task lighting with an industrial look, an antique iron chandelier provides ambience.

Squeezed-in breakfast room. A bistro table and two leather folding chairs offer a place to sip coffee with a sidewalk-cafe feel.

farmhouse chic

Vertical boards on walls and island and rustic finishes set a country tone.

Why it works:

Fresh approach to the bar. Pushing a farm table against the island keeps the around-the-table-family-meal tradition. A downsized pair of stools mimics the barstool silhouette.

Handsome palette. The rich cocoa paint color of the drawers and cabinets is repeated on the window sashes and complemented by the wood tones of the farm table. The contrasting creamy white used in the rest of the space makes the room feel light and open.

Sculptural pieces. The quartz CaesarStone® that wraps the sides of the island protects it from daily bumps and dings and also gives it a sleek profile. The horse's head, vent hood, butcher-block backsplash behind the cooktop, and angular island fixture all add to the sculptural appeal.

hip *and* modern

Kitchen of artist, clothing designer,
and photographer Alyson Fox
Austin, Texas

Why it works:

Out with the same old-same old. A
daring use of wood planks for the open
shelving and cabinetry is refreshingly different. "We wanted a space that was a nice
balance of masculine and feminine—nothing
too sparse, but nothing too girlie," says the
homeowner, Alyson Fox.

Organic mingles with industrial. A mix
of wood, stainless steel appliances, and a
stainless steel backsplash create contrasting
surfaces that complement each other. Instead
of upper cabinets, shelves of Microllam®
(strips of wood glued together and laminated)
are hung on hidden brackets and keep daily
tabletop accessories within reach.

Brave color. To contrast the lightly stained
maple base cabinetry, a striking red-orange
paint was added to the cabinets adjacent to
the sink and cooktop, providing the finishing
touch that makes the space memorable.

> **We had fun creating different looks with stainless steel and wood,** says Fox.

designer cue

An Internet search under "antique Magic Chef stove" will bring up a wealth of information on dealers of these antique appliances, as well as resources for parts needed to undertake a restoration project of this kind.

primitive

Kitchen of artists Mary Cooper and
Tomio Thomann, New Orleans, Louisiana

Why it works:

Everything in full view. Nothing hides behind a cabinet here, and the practical and artful solution to limited space in the cupboard results in a graphic arrangement of pots and pans.

Restored utilities. A Magic Chef® gas stove from the 1930s fills a narrow kitchen niche. The sink (found abandoned on the side of the road) was purchased from a local nonprofit salvage company and restored.

Authentic Creole. The house was recently restored to its original state—including the vibrant blue color of the kitchen. The baseboards are a flat Spanish brown, typical in Creole houses.

concealed utilitarian
Kitchen of designer Mary Evelyn McKee
Birmingham, Alabama

designer cue

Standard countertop thickness is about 1 inch. Doubling or even tripling the thickness, as seen here, can add drama and richness to your kitchen. It's expensive, though, so consider applying the idea to one area, like the island or just around the range, to avoid exorbitant costs.

Why it works:

Seamless room-to-room flow. Sleek lines draw the eye beyond the kitchen to the library's traditional furnishings. "In the morning, sunlight bounces in through the library and casts a wonderful wavy light in the kitchen," says designer Mary Evelyn McKee. A thick butcher-block top downplays the utilitarian role of the island, making it appear more like a piece of furniture.

Hidden clutter. Clean countertops are a product of having a place for everything in a large drawer, a cabinet, or behind a stainless screen that rolls up and down to access essentials.

Neutral palette. A mix of whites from the wall color, countertops, cabinetry, and bookshelves in both rooms leaves the transition uninterrupted. The only color needed to accent both rooms comes from the wall of books.

casual sophistication

Why it works:

Pretty furnishings. Barstools were designed as two-seater settees, upholstered in the style of living room furniture. A collection of mortar and pestle pieces adds visual interest. An abundance of houseplants and herbs soften the somewhat industrial look.

Not-so-serious architecture. Added during a renovation, traces of the past, a painted brick wall as a backsplash, and sunlight diffused by a sheer-curtained skylight harken back to the days when this was a backyard courtyard.

Island as furniture. Designed with carved legs, the island is reminiscent of a dining table. A built-in cabinet cleverly tucked underneath provides extra storage while still leaving legroom for guests sitting on barstools.

Kitchen islands have been the workhorse of the kitchen for centuries. Nowadays, they serve multiple functions as prep area, dining table, serving station, and work surface. See how Southerners approach this hub of the home.

(An island "on the go" can be helpful all around the kitchen.)

(A petite table and chairs extend this island's length and work as a spot for tea.)

(Consider a table and chairs instead.)

(The 5-foot peninsula provides an ideal spot to grab a quick bite. It can also serve as a buffet and bar for entertaining.)

fresh ideas: *discovering sink solutions*

> **❝I love to use silver sinks and farm sinks. To me, they are classic.**

You still see them being used in the oldest farmhouses in Europe. They are perfectly timeless,❞ says Birmingham, Alabama, kitchen designer Cindy Cantley.

(The depth and width of a farm sink make it adaptable to multiple uses.)

(Consider the opportunity to surprise with the color of your sink.)

(Instead of a newly designed sink, this homeowner used a farmhouse-style with a fluted front apron. The retro-look wall-mounted faucet helps preserve the integrity of the 1940s-era kitchen.)

(When entertaining, the homeowner fills one side of this sink with ice to keep bottles of wine and Champagne chilled.)

take it from *Cindy:*

On countertops: 1.) My favorite surface for kitchens is honed marble for a classic, never-trendy look. Yes, it will stain, but that's part of its charm. **2.)** Black walnut is great as an accent surface, but it's pricey, so consider using it in small doses on an island or either side of the range. It's surprisingly heat and stain resistant. **3.)** Soapstone won't burn or stain, and it requires little maintenance. It does go dark over time, and it must be oiled, depending on use. **4.)** I prefer honed over polished granite—honing gives a new look to this popular surface. It works best in a contemporary setting; it tends to be a little modern for classic kitchens. **5.)** I love the thickness of limestone, and it makes a statement on a center island. I like to seal it with beeswax. Its neutral color complements any interior. It will stain, but it develops an alluring patina.

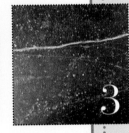

1   2   3   4   5

fresh ideas: *creating a breakfast area*

Look beyond the usual table and chairs to sofas, upholstered pieces, built-ins, and furnishings that serve multiple functions. Let these Southern nooks inspire you.

(This custom settee has the feel of a built-in, but it can be picked up and moved anywhere. No children in the house minimized the need for an extra-durable fabric, so the owner chose a snappy, plaid wool.)

(The cushions on a pair of built-in benches are covered in easy-care vinyl to accommodate spills. Drawers underneath provide extra storage for large items.)

(A bistro-like dining area in this tiny kitchen pulls right up to the open bookshelves. The homeowner treated the wooden tabletop with polyurethane to protect it during daily use.)

(A traditional sofa gives this nook more of a living room feel, but the shocking pink covering makes it the hot spot for breakfast.)

fresh ideas: *disguising appliances*

Revealed or concealed, stow away the accoutrements of the kitchen in traditional or more inventive, contemporary ways as seen in these inspired spaces.

(This refrigerator closes to look like a piece of finely crafted furniture.)

(The refrigerator and freezer drawers disappear into the wall.)

(The pantry pulls out to reveal spices and other cooking essentials and closes to look like a vertical cabinet.)

and pantry spaces

(Family-photo doors conceal this built-in china cabinet with its copper accents.)

Personalize your kitchen with beloved collections, convenient accessories for storage and style, and a dose of the unexpected to lend interest to a utilitarian room used every day.

(Cabinets inset with glass reveal collected serving pieces and pretty glassware.)

(Remove unsightly cabinet doors for instant open shelving.)

(A mirror over the range is an unexpected touch that adds a bright spot of natural light.)

(A ledge and two alcoves near the stove keep spices, oils, and utensils handy.)

backsplash *(details)*

(marble)

(marble mosaic)

(marble tile)

(glass)

(glass mosaic)

(old-world)

(subway tile)

(beaded board)

(marble) Using the same material on both the backsplash and counter surface creates a seamless effect. Here, marble subway tiles are laid in a herringbone pattern.

(marble mosaic) Marble mosaic tile applied in a herringbone pattern gives a bold, graphic look.

(marble tile) Custom-cut marble subway tiles contrast a stainless steel countertop with a 4-inch lip that works with the backsplash to protect the walls.

(glass) Glass subway tiles accent this white kitchen.

(glass mosaic) Here, 1- by 2-inch glass mosaic tiles complement, rather than match, the cabinet color.

(old-world) This subway-tile backsplash is finished around the edges with a 1-inch pencil liner.

(subway tile) Subway tiles are probably the most commonly used style. Named after the style of tile originally installed in New York subways, its standard size is a 3- by 6-inch brick-like shape, but it comes in a variety of versions.

(beaded board) Cottage-style beaded board covers the walls from counter to ceiling.

pulling it all together:

choose the...

Cabinet style. Distinguishing between painted wood or stained (or if you're a modernist, laminate or stainless steel) is the first decision. After that, choose custom or stock. If budget is key, then stock cabinets are the way to go though there's little wiggle room on dimensions—all the cabinets and drawers will be standard sizes. Custom cabinets cost more, but the options are endless.

Either comes in a variety of styles, from flat, sleek fronts for contemporary looks to raised or inset panels (some with glass) for the traditionalist. Many custom cabinets are inset, flush with the casing, and some have hidden hinges; stock cabinets are typically overlaid. In both cases, hanging upper cabinets at the ceiling can enhance room size.

apply...

Hardware. Knobs, pulls, and latches should complement the style and finish of the cabinet. Latches with an antique finish more commonly invoke a traditional bungalow style.

Angular-designed pulls with shiny finishes work well with a modern design. If you're sticking with existing cabinetry, simply changing the hardware can give an instant new look.

select...

Sink faucet. Although modern-style faucets can make a statement by arching dramatically over the sink, when selecting plumbing fixtures, keep your cabinet hardware in mind.

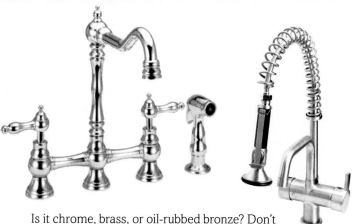

Is it chrome, brass, or oil-rubbed bronze? Don't stray too far, though—it typically looks best to match (or complement) finishes throughout the kitchen.

top with...

Counters. Choices include solid wood (best used as an accent), a slab of stone (for a durable, clean look), or a mosaic of tiles (for an old-fashioned, cottage style).

The standard depth is 25 inches—consider something deeper if you have a short span of counterspace.

It's often nice to mix it up with one material on the island and another on the countertops.

add...

Appliances. Industrial-looking appliances are all the rage, but if you're just not a cook, forgo the cost of an expensive gas range—a cooktop (even electric) can look just as chic.

And while stainless steel appliances tend to easily adapt to the colors and styles of most interiors, more colorful options have hit the market—though going that route makes your interiors less flexible to change. Small appliances in bright accent colors are a better choice if you have a commitment phobia.

enhance with...

Lighting. Task lighting is key to a functional kitchen. Pendants work best for concentrated light in the areas where you do most prep work, like the island; two pendants or one large fixture generally will do the trick over a standard-size island. Flush-mounted lighting gives the best overall ambience.

center with...

An island (and barstools). Sizes vary, but the general recommended distance between the closest counter-top and the island is 36 inches. Use your imagination to tailor it to your specific needs: Use it as a prep spot, mount your sink or cooktop on it, or fill it with drawers and cabinets for extra storage. It can be built in, on wheels, or simply a large table-like piece used as a dining spot, in which case barstools or chairs are essential. Choose a barstool style that works with your decor, but if guests will sit for long periods, opt for a seat with a back.

dining rooms

Once thought of as the most formal room in the house, the dining room has evolved, like every other space, with the casualness of modern family life. In the Old South, dining rooms were elaborate spaces for entertaining. Back then, there were no real "metropolises" filled with restaurant choices for fine foods and cocktails served in elegant settings. Social occasions were typically held at home—hence, the finely decorated dining room to impress and welcome guests. Today, the region is scattered with cities that offer a wide array of options for social dining away from home.

Even though over-the-top glamour (sometimes dubbed "stuffy" by younger generations) in the dining room remains a Southern tradition, less-formal entertaining and multipurpose use for the space has taken hold. Some homeowners decline a designated dining room altogether and set aside a corner in the kitchen or another room with a table and chairs instead. Some dining rooms even assume the role of a home office when the table is not set. Nonetheless, so many personal interpretations of this place in the modern home have initiated countless, stylish solutions for making it work for today's lifestyle while keeping it beautifully rooted in tradition.

A perfect combination of formal and comfortable, this dining room still shows pedigreed touches—a crystal chandelier, an oversize antique table, and old-fashioned cane-back chairs—mixed among potted ferns and new chairs from a mail-order catalog. "Overscale pieces keep the rooms from looking prissy or staid," says designer Janie Molster, pointing out the extra-long dining table.

"I could live in a modern glass house or a French château. I go from one extreme to the other, and I love contrasts," explains Houston designer Katie Stassi. "I just blend everything so it flows. "

château meets chic

Dining room of designer Katie Stassi
Houston, Texas

Why it works:

One-color scheme. Using one main color on the large pieces—the blue-green banquette and mirror—keeps the look clean and simple. Accenting with a contrasting shade—in this case, the white chairs, table, and sconces—makes the room easily interchangeable.

Swapability. The slipcovered banquette has a custom built-in feel, but it can easily go to another room. For homeowners who like to frequently switch things around, it's best to consider versatility when making decorating decisions.

Daring mix of old and new. An antique French mirror looks right at home with the slipcovered banquette, sleek glass-topped table, and iconic Eames side chairs.

comfortably elegant

Dining room of decorator Carolyn Malone, Atlanta, Georgia

Why it works:

Unpretentious twists. "I love European influence," says Atlanta decorator Carolyn Malone, "but I cannot shed the relaxed and inviting ways of the South." Here, she takes antique chairs down a notch, slip-covering them in white muslin. "Slipcovers make for less stress with children, dogs, and, some-times, husbands—swift removal, cleaning, and back on," says Malone.

Formal with a wink. This room has a sense of formality, yet elements with a sense of humor are welcoming, like the not-your-typical lime green walls that play off the garden, an antique bust perched unexpectedly atop a bistro table, and the chipped paint of the china cabinet.

Bare floor. Embrace the wear and tear. "You are talking to someone who does not have a rug in her own house," says Malone.

texture

take it from *Carolyn:*

Fabric choices play a key role in making formal rooms comfortable. "I like all natural—linen, velvet, washed linen, or block-printed cotton or silk." **1.)** Natural fabrics make great curtains. **2.)** They are favorites of mine for skirted slipcovers on chairs. **3.)** They are also versatile choices for tufted covers on long benches. **4.)** A block print can be handsome, mellow, and a bit modern.

designer cue

The average height of a dining table is 28 to 30 inches, and chair seats are generally 11 to 13 inches beneath table height. The higher the tabletop, the more uncomfortable and formal the table feels. In this case the lower table (28 inches) better accommodates the low-slung sofa. FYI: When entertaining, it's customary to allow at least 24 inches of elbow room for each guest and 12- to 15-inches depth from the edge of the table.

traditional twist

Dining room of shopkeeper Christy Ford, Charlottesville, Virginia

Why it works:

Practicality rules. A bleachable, white slipcover easily accommodates spills and other mishaps on this comfortable seating, which is paired with a slightly lowered English tea table. Loosely arranged china in the corner cabinet is convenient for setting the table on the spot.

Subtly layered. Painted furniture, a leopard-print rug, and a series of botanicals decorating the walls add understated depth to this room by keeping a subdued color palette—rich browns, soft whites, and gentle blues.

Yin and Yang. Traditional furnishings—dining chairs, a buffet, and a china cabinet—all masked with coats of flaky paint pair nicely with a modern animal-print rug. A chandelier predictably placed in the middle of the room is surprisingly crafted of horns.

formal flair

Dining room designed by Richard Keith Langham, Palm Beach, Florida

Why it works:

Unleashed imagination. The coral and white *parapluie* overhead was handmade using strips of fabric and fitted to the ceiling. Think it looks like an umbrella? *Parapluie* is the French word for umbrella.

Sense of place. Not only the soft blues and muted sunset colors hint at the room's coastal locale—accents, like a pair of coral sconces enhanced with brass seahorses, also do the trick.

Bold shapes. A round table (fun to crowd people around), graphic painted chairs, and a fanciful chandelier embellished with stars signal a backdrop for lavish entertaining.

inside out

Dining room of shopkeeper
Cynthia Davis, Houston, Texas

Why it works:

Rain or shine furnishings. An outdoor ceiling fixture as a chandelier
and an iron table base topped with glass and paired with woven dining
chairs are stylish enough to decorate this interior room, yet versatile
enough to move outside to the garden.

Architectural connections. Three glass-paneled doors, instead of
windows, open to the patio, creating a seamless indoor/outdoor feel.
Simple garden border tiles along the floorboard (see inset photo above)
also subtly underscore the connection to the garden.

Natural accents. Potted lavender, rosemary, and ivy further reflect the
green outside and are easy to maintain indoors.

bordered beauty

10

designer cue

After you've chosen a paint color, buy a pint (many stores offer sample sizes) to do a test patch. Paint a big square of plywood or poster board with the color, and place it directly against the wall. Look at it at all times of day—morning, midday, and night—to see how it reflects the light. Let it dry fully before making a decision (wet paint looks different from dry), and keep in mind that the current color in the room may be reflecting off it. If so, find a neutral spot in a different room that has a similar amount of light exposure to do that test.

alternative glamour

Dining room by decorator Kim Zimmerman, Atlanta, Georgia

Why it works:

Guts with color. Set off by an unexpected turquoise palette, traditional antiques seamlessly unite with modern art. Atlanta decorator Kim Zimmerman tested the color several times before she found the right shade, and then she heightened the energy by painting a set of vintage bamboo dining chairs in the same hue.

Not-so-ordinary art. A vibrant nod to the owner's love of music, a collection of pop art prints, featuring each member of the popular Beatles group, punctuates the wall.

Touch of tradition. The portraits hang prominently behind an antique oak dining table. For pet birds Fiddle and Faddle, a vintage ornate birdcage makes a big impact as one of the few accessories in the room.

fresh ideas: *arranging dining rooms*

More versatile than ever before, this isn't your grandmother's traditional seating for six. Inventive solutions for a room that seldom gets daily use bring the dining room to new heights.

(A group of comfy upholstered chairs provides an alternative to traditional, delicate wooden dining chairs.)

(Big furniture and an oversize chandelier in a small room play up the coziness.)

(Avoid "matchy-matchy" by placing host and hostess chairs in a different style at the head and foot of the table.)

(When the table is not set for entertaining, use it to display books and accessories for an interesting day-to-day look.)

(Iron folding chairs, meant for the garden, look fitting in a room with a wall of paneless windows that show off the backyard.)

(A decorative vinyl "hat" that can be removed and cleaned protects an inherited, antique table from spills.)

china cabinet *(details)*

(After the table, the china cabinet is typically the most prominent piece in the dining room. This one, built in the style of an old kitchen hutch with a lower unit of cabinets and drawers and a set of shelves or cabinets placed on top, hints at a time when actual pieces of furniture, instead of built-in cabinets and pantries, housed everything. Today, a hutch is often used in the dining room in place of a more formal china cabinet. This one was custom designed with ample storage and other inventive uses in mind.)

(kitchen hutch)

(chippendale)

(reproduction)

(built-in)

(corner cupboard)

(antique cabinet)

(kitchen hutch) Not only to store necessities, they can also hold a ready-for-entertaining bar with a built-in sink.

(chippendale) A classic Chippendale china cabinet gets an updated look when it is placed in front of graphic wallpaper and filled with colorful china.

(reproduction) A coat of white paint hides flaws in once-dated and worn woodwork to give this cabinet a stylish look. Cool idea: Replace the glass with mirrors for added glamour.

(built-in) A twist on the typical freestanding piece, this one is built into the wall. Old French doors expose the china inside.

(corner cupboard) An antique corner cupboard with open shelves serves as a china cabinet in a tiny dining room, where space is limited.

(antique cabinet) The homeowner found this antique cabinet and had a furniture maker build the bottom to match. Milk paint brightens the original mahogany finish.

pulling it all together:

start with...

Dining table. Size matters; make sure the table allows 30 to 36 inches around the perimeter for walking and scooting chairs back. Think about how the table will be used: Not everyone hosts 20 people for dinner, but some people do. A 60-inch diameter round table will seat up to 10 people, and nothing encourages dinner conversation more than a **round table**.

A little more traditional is the **oval table**, which has the length but not the hard edges of a standard-size, 36- by 72-inch rectangular table, which comfortably seats eight people.

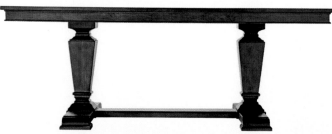

The long, narrow shape of a **rectangular table** plays on a room's length, maximizing the space and making it look larger.

surround with...

Chairs. Choose a style that fits the environment as well as the scale and design of the table. The seat height of a traditional chair is typically 18 inches—a nice proportion if the table is the standard 29 inches high.

In some cases, a chair does not necessarily need to be in the same style as the table. A **modern acrylic chair**, in contrast to a traditional table, would work in an eclectic setting. It is also easy to clean, a crucial consideration if children are frequent diners.

Mixed arrangements, like a **bench** or a **settee** on one side of the table with chairs on the other, is another alternative.

top with a...

Chandelier. Simple rules of thumb: The width of the chandelier should be 12 inches narrower than the width of the table. Most chandeliers should hang 30 to 34 inches above the table surface—make sure it's not too tall to be hung high enough.

If you're in the market for a chandelier, the options are endless, ranging from **peculiar objects**, such as fishing baskets turned upside and wired, to **outdoor lanterns** that complement casual, rustic interiors.

Of course, you can go the no-fail traditional look with six to eight arms of candle-like light.

add a...

Buffet. The dining room is typically in close proximity to the party, so a piece of furniture is needed to serve the food as well as house special-occasion dishes, tableware, and linens. A **buffet sideboard** is usually 36 inches high with two doors that open to reveal storage and a couple of drawers.

Styles vary from **doors only** to **open consoles** with a few drawers, which are especially helpful for people who also have a china cabinet for extra storage or simply want to keep special things arranged in full view.

consider a...

Bar. When entertaining, it's nice to top the buffet with pretty accessories as a spot for the **bar.** Or, if your dining room is big enough, a **bar cart** can be a versatile, movable station.

bedrooms

Perhaps no space in the home is more personal than the bedroom, a favored retreat for rest or quiet moments. While the comfort factor is most important—a bed with a mattress that supports and cradles the body, pillows that cushion the head and neck, and crisp linens that are soft to the touch—the style quotient also looms large.

Traditional Southern bedrooms call to mind the rooms our ancestors loved, complete with four-poster beds, canopies dressed in yards of fabric, abundant floral prints skirting the beds and covering the windows, and the generous use of ruffles, swags, and pleats. Today's modern styles do not lose sight of comfort and serenity, yet the look is more streamlined, with graphic upholstered headboards, simple bed dressings, contemporary art, sea grass rugs, and unexpected touches like a color that seems improbable or a pattern that shakes things up a bit. In all its incarnations, however, the bedroom is a most private world, where stacks of books reveal our interests, photographs tell our personal history, and color and fabric choices divulge the palette and motifs that soothe and shield us from the outside world.

(Left) A new campaign-style canopy bed contrasts with rustic timber walls. The white linens accentuate the contrast, while the lilac silk softens the space. Historically, Southerners draped sheer cotton netting from the ceiling to provide protection from mosquitoes coming in from open windows. Here, sheers evoke that long-ago tradition, now as an accent rather than a necessity.

haute hippie

Bedroom by designer Amelia Handegan
Charleston, South Carolina

Why it works:

A single showpiece. An embroidered suzani—a decorative Afghan textile—functions as a bedspread, livens up the neutral room, and can be switched out easily.

Lopsided architecture. An oddly angled room squares up with a grouping of art and walls upholstered in simple ticking. A dark trim border creates definition.

Mismatched meets symmetry. Random nightstands—which are not part of a pair—suit the room's overall mood and vintage style, while a pair of matching lamps balances the space and gives it a sense of maturity.

fashion forward

designer cue

For a more subtle take on the industrial look shown here, try painting the walls, ductwork, and exposed brick all the same color.

Why it works:

Exposed elements. Exposed ductwork and electrical wiring, a brick wall, plus bare floors leave nothing to the imagination and provide a surprising contrast to a mix of antique and modern furnishings.

Loads of art. Black frames, in varying styles, unify a combination of art prints and photographs of all shapes and sizes.

Stylish furnishings. The very modern silhouette of this platform bed is toned down when it is covered in a natural sea grass fabric and surrounded by traditional elements like the dainty end table, a pair of French chairs, and a fanciful iron garden bench.

sumptuous and serene

Bedroom by designer Dan Carithers
Atlanta, Georgia

Why it works:

Two-tone contrasts. Shades of brown paired with crisp white linens amid traditional furniture, lighting, and a luxe faux fur create a sense of harmony. Dark chocolate molding (a departure from the typical white) coordinates with elements in the room, like the headboard, furniture, and prints on the wall.

Artful symmetry. Framed prints follow the lines of the headboard to create balance in the room. For fun, the designer used fixtures installed in the ceiling rather than predictable art lights hung on the wall.

Personalization. Though a white-on-white monogram is the most traditional, the modern style makes a bold statement.

designer cue

Upholstered walls are an ideal way to camouflage awkward room proportions and also—with a layer of batting underneath—absorb sound. If you find a fabric that you'd rather use as wallpaper, ask about having it paper-backed. There is a charge for the backing, but the labor cost of hanging it like wallpaper can be less expensive than actually upholstering the walls.

cottage refinement

Bedroom of designer Mary Evelyn McKee
Birmingham, Alabama

Why it works:

Profusion of pattern. Making the most of a quirky roofline, a block-print fabric covers the walls and eaves, serving as a canopy over the bed. "The pattern softens all those angles and blurs the edges of the room," says Birmingham designer Mary Evelyn McKee.

Snug effect. Nestling the bed under the eaves creates a cocoon-like feel that lends to the room's comfortable appeal. Oversize lamps exaggerate the drama of the diminutive square footage.

Antique textiles. Mostly thought of for more formal spaces, throw pillows made of old textiles decorate the bed in this room, tying in other antique furnishings.

relaxed approach

Bedroom of shopkeeper Cynthia Davis, Houston, Texas

Why it works:

Garden gateway. French doors open directly into the garden, and house-plants accentuate the indoor/outdoor feel.

Mix of textures. Instead of color, natural textures define this space: wall-to-wall sea grass; baskets at the foot of the bed, turned upside down as a television stand, and holding books and remotes by the nightstand; sheer, gauzy curtains tied to rods; and a bench with a natural rush-woven seat.

Dramatic headboard. Graphic curves and a whopping height—almost to the top of the windows—make the headboard the room's showstopper.

take it from *Cynthia:*

"It's our best-seller," says Cynthia Davis, the owner of Indulge, a shop known for European linens and other home accents. "This headboard makes such a statement. You don't want other pieces competing with it as a focal point." She's seen the headboard in a number of interpretations—pink with white trim makes it girlie, while various shades of linen with nail head trim seems more masculine.

color act

Bedroom designed by Celerie Kemble
Palm Beach, Florida

Why it works:

Color as a neutral. "Pale green is very much a neutral," says designer Celerie Kemble. "Green is omnipresent in the natural world, and our eyes are comfortable accepting a lot of it." She enveloped this space in the color as much as possible. "The more of it you put in a room, the less it feels like a jolt of color, and the more it feels like a spring backdrop," she notes.

Overuse of pattern. To add more visual punch, Kemble layered patterns—checks, stripes, and dots. "That continuity keeps it interesting but still restful and serene," she says. She started with the striped wallpaper and had a faux finisher glaze the trim in a slightly deeper shade.

Want-to-curl-up vibe. Using an oversize upholstered headboard and adding striped wallpaper to the ceiling diminishes the size of the room, giving it a cozy feel. Built-in shelves loaded with books give a reason to burrow beneath the covers.

designer cue

Notice the snug fit of the bedspread. Form-fitting the bedspread to the mattress is a clean and tailored approach that makes for short-and-sweet bed making.

down-to-earth chic

Guest room of shopkeeper Amy Gardner
Charlottesville, Virginia

Why it works:

Recycled materials. Reclaimed oak from a cider mill in England partially covers the walls and also acts as the headboard, warming the off-white paint color and concrete floors. Once a porch, this room already had a concrete floor, and with a little polish and stain, there was no need to replace it.

Simplicity. A bed with no frame, a wooden box as side table, and a primitive pine dresser offer a simple yet chic approach to decorating.

Up-to-the-minute style. Throwing in a cowhide rug and a mid-century modern-style chair with chrome arms and legs pushes the style quotient off the charts.

designer cue

Notice the snug fit of the bedspread. Form-fitting the bedspread to the mattress is a clean and tailored approach that makes for short-and-sweet bed making.

down-to-earth chic

Guest room of shopkeeper Amy Gardner
Charlottesville, Virginia

Why it works:

Recycled materials. Reclaimed oak from a cider mill in England partially covers the walls and also acts as the headboard, warming the off-white paint color and concrete floors. Once a porch, this room already had a concrete floor, and with a little polish and stain, there was no need to replace it.

Simplicity. A bed with no frame, a wooden box as side table, and a primitive pine dresser offer a simple yet chic approach to decorating.

Up-to-the-minute style. Throwing in a cowhide rug and a mid-century modern-style chair with chrome arms and legs pushes the style quotient off the charts.

designer cue

Notice the snug fit of the bedspread. Form-fitting the bedspread to the mattress is a clean and tailored approach that makes for short-and-sweet bed making.

down-to-earth chic
Guest room of shopkeeper Amy Gardner
Charlottesville, Virginia

Why it works:

Recycled materials. Reclaimed oak from a cider mill in England partially covers the walls and also acts as the headboard, warming the off-white paint color and concrete floors. Once a porch, this room already had a concrete floor, and with a little polish and stain, there was no need to replace it.

Simplicity. A bed with no frame, a wooden box as side table, and a primitive pine dresser offer a simple yet chic approach to decorating.

Up-to-the-minute style. Throwing in a cowhide rug and a mid-century modern-style chair with chrome arms and legs pushes the style quotient off the charts.

ooh-la-la style

Bedroom of designer and
shopkeeper Lee Kleinhelter
Atlanta, Georgia

Why it works:

Solid paint and upholstery. Ceiling, walls,
and trim all got a coat of dark paint, which is
further accentuated by curtains in the same
dark color. "I use a lot of solid upholstery,"
says Lee Kleinhelter. "I keep the pattern
in things like custom pillows. I'm always
changing my interior, so it's nice to have a
neutral background to do that."

High-impact accessories. A few accents
of yellow—a pair of lamps and a decorative
pillow—make a bold impression on the
overall look of the room. They can be easily
interchanged with another color to give an
entirely different look.

Show-it-all nightstands. Nothing is hidden
behind drawers on these end tables, with
ample open shelving holding everything from
books to alarm clocks.

designer cue

A traditional chandelier becomes more
hip with small round bulbs instead of
the usual candle-shaped ones.

fresh ideas: *four-poster beds*

Stately four-poster beds are seen in many Southern homes. A hundred years ago, they were dressed and dripping in fabric. Today, we often see them bare and sculptural, or if fabric is involved, it's often a play on traditional treatments.

(A canopy bed, a cousin to the four-poster, gets an understated, simple sheet of fabric tied around the edges across the top.)

(Mosquito netting, the most traditional material for cocooning a four-poster bed, drapes from rings fixed to the ceiling over this Louisiana rolling pin bed and accentuates the height of the room.)

(The sharp contrast of colors on the curtain panels at the corners of this iron canopy bed can be reversed for a change of pace.)

(There are actually no posts at all, but a rod attached to the ceiling and dressed with curtain panels at the four corners creates the illusion of a four-poster bed.)

(Canopies left bare grab attention in otherwise subtle rooms with minimal decor.)

fresh ideas: *closet spaces*

More than a space to simply stow stuff, today closets are outfitted like rooms with lighting, mirrors, seating, and well-designed storage.

(No need to dig through a box—a bulletin board covered in chic fabric hangs jewelry artfully in plain view.)

(Everyday accessories like scarves, handbags, and jewelry are treated like decorative items, adding splashes of color to the white tableau.)

(A cushy daybed gives a front-row view through the glass closet doors, eliminating the need for scrambling around to find shoes and accessories.)

(Posting snapshots on the outside of shoe boxes reveals what's inside.)

(This closet conveniently accommodates the washer and dryer. Dark walls help the couple's clothes stand out so it's easier to find things.)

bed *(details)*

(The bed is the most important element of the room, so consider what best fits your style. The canopy bed came into existence for utilitarian reasons rather than the extravagance it's known for today. The earliest versions were probably beds of common people who were seeking shelter under mosquito netting. Noblemen added luxurious curtains for warmth and privacy. This iron canopy, left unadorned, makes an architectural statement in this rather sparse room. Draped in fabric, it would take on a more feminine look.)

(corona)

(upholstered)

(screen)

(rolling pin style)

(baroque)

(sleigh)

(corona) Regal coronas originated as baldachins that held decorative flourishes above thrones and other "high" places. Today, new or antique, coronas often anchor draped fabric over the bed, swagged with hardware tiebacks.

(upholstered) Relatively inexpensive and easy to customize (any silhouette can be covered with batting and fabric stapled into place), upholstered headboards provide soft texture and cushy spots for reading.

(screen) No need for art when a custom or antique screen serves as the headboard.

(rolling pin style) These prized antiques are most often seen in four-poster versions. As twin beds with lower posts, they work great in a guest room.

(baroque) An elaborately carved wooden frame maintains opulence with a tufted upholstered center made of rich red fabric.

(sleigh) Curved at the head and foot, resembling a horse-drawn sleigh, these beds are traditionally made from wood, but the newer upholstered ones are quite comfortable. Put one sleigh bed in the middle of the room as a stand-alone piece, or push a twin-size one against the wall as a daybed.

pulling it all together:

start with a...

Mattress.
Always try out a
mattress by lying down on
it in a normal sleep position. Mattress choices vary
among pillow-tops, which offer extra softness but are
not made to be flipped (they can be rotated clockwise
every few months to even out wear); memory foams,
which conform to your body; inner springs, which
refer to coil counts or the number of springs inside
(the higher the number, the better); and latex mat-
tresses, which are coil free. Replace your mattress
every 7 to 10 years. If you see indentations after you
flip it, it's time for a new one.

add...

Linens and pillows. Pillows filled with 100% white
goose down are considered premium, although a
mix of feathers and down has a firmer consistency.
The pillow casing should be at least 200 thread count
to keep the feathers from poking through. Cotton-
filled pillows are a better option for people with
allergies.

A sheet **thread count** of 200 and above is considered good quality—from 250 to 400, you can
generally tell a difference. A good-quality sheet
should last 5 to 10 years, especially if you don't
overbleach it, which weakens
the fibers. Consider using a
generous-size flat sheet
(buy it one size up) instead
of a fitted one; it conforms
easily to the newer,
thicker mattress styles,
and fitted sheets tend
to wear out from the
pulling and stretching
of frequent changes.

flank with...

Nightstands. Identical nightstands
flanking the bed provide symmetry and traditionalism, but bedside
tables don't have to match. They
should, however, stand taller than
the mattress. A small chest with
drawers keeps odds and ends concealed, but if something less heavy
looks best, an open nightstand with
one small drawer works well; for
extra storage, try placing a basket
underneath the nightstand. For twin
beds, a shared table between the
beds is a smart use of space.

add a...

Reading light. Sconces require installing, but they are the most effective way to get good light. As a general guideline, the bottom of the shade should be 42 inches above the floor.

Swing-arm sconces. These give the most direct light. Table lamps work great as pairs on nightstands.

For a reading lamp, consider using opaque shades to help direct the light; place a large translucent shade on a lamp that will be used as a significant light source.

place a...

Bench, chaise, settee, or even two chairs at the foot of the bed to complete the look and add additional space to store reading material, drape a jacket, or just curl up with a book.

bathrooms

A room doesn't get much more utilitarian than the bathroom. Nonetheless, whether it's a guest bath for weekend visitors or the sanctuary of a master bath, Southerners have taken the space beyond merely functional and elevated the style in distinctive ways, including unique uses of color, sleek designs in sinks and faucets, and tasteful choices of tiles in all shapes and sizes.

While classic subway tiles, beaded board, and pedestal sinks are still prevalent, the modern bath holds many surprises, like a sink set into an antique chest for a vanity, materials salvaged from European sources for the floor and walls, and the much-loved claw-foot tub glamorously updated with nickel plating.

(Right) This English Mastiff, named Mabel, enjoys cooling off in the deep nickel-plated tub. Gray-and-ivory striped curtains frame the windows in the sun-filled room.

designer cue

Cuban encaustic tiles are found in many 1920s South Florida homes. Encaustic indicates that the pattern is part of the material, rather than being applied or painted on, so it remains intact, no matter the wear and tear. These tiles are considered "green" because most are produced using natural earth pigments. If you worry that the cement might be hard on your feet, consider using the tiles as a backsplash or wainscot for added color.

pretty in pink

Bathroom of magazine editor Carey Winfrey
Key West, Florida

Why it works:

Renovated, 2005—Looks like 1920. Once historic elements
are removed, they're gone forever. The owners of this historic Key West
cottage saved the original claw-foot tub by resurfacing it. They added
colorful Cuban floor tiles, which are commonly seen in old Florida homes.

Prissy attitude. Pale pink walls play off the color in the floor tiles. A
delicate wire wall-mounted storage rack casually holds essentials mixed
with framed art.

Freestanding tub with shower. Vintage style need not eliminate the
modern shower when wall-mounted (shown here), rim-mounted, or freestanding hardware is used.

uptown utilitarian

Bathroom of Atlanta natives Ginny and Craig
Magher in the South of France

Why it works:

Living room furniture in the bath. An elegant trumeau mirror (not your typical medicine cabinet look) flanked by fanciful sconces hangs above a marble-top antique table, which serves as the vanity. A pair of lamps with extended candle arms heightens the old-world feel.

Open storage. Going with the antique table left bath towels on display, not hidden in a cabinet. Folded neatly with the monograms on top, they add to the decor, not to mention they are easy to access.

Masculine elegance. Wood tones and black accents stand out against the white walls, which helps downplay the prettiness of the mirror with its painting of a hunting hound.

white haute style

Master bath of decorator Heidi Friedler
New Orleans, Louisiana

Why it works:

An explosion of white. This bath is pure white—stained wood floors, painted plank walls and trim, marble countertops, pleated valance, and crystal lamps—no exceptions.

Defining shapes. The absence of contrasting color emphasizes the graphic shapes that define the room—the round mirrors above the rectangular-shaped vanities with round crystal pulls, the sleek profile of the freestanding tub, and the spiral twisting of the modern ceiling fixture.

His-and-her vanities. Many master baths have double sinks, but double vanities are a real treat (notice the feet made to look like furniture). "His" has more open storage, while "hers" has more drawers.

simply luxurious

Master bath of Katherine and Ashley Hefner
Beaufort, South Carolina

Why it works:

Minimalism to the max. An excessive amount of 1- by 1-inch golden glass tiles surrounding the base and covering the walls around the tub creates a uniform look. Salvaged wood with a light stain on the ceiling enhances the color of the tiles.

Improvised storage solution. An old wooden ladder is an imaginative choice for storing towels and other bath essentials.

Painted floor. Creamy off-white paint coats the wood floor, providing a clean palette in keeping with the walls, trim, and variations in the tiles. Leaving the original dark stain on the floor would have created an entirely different look.

designer cue

Be sure to use a polyurethane seal as the last step in painting a wooden bathroom floor to protect it from water and steam, which it's not normally exposed to in other rooms.

salvaged serenity

Master bath of Cynthia Davis, Houston, Texas

Why it works:

Bathed in texture. A sheer shower curtain (a hidden rod is mounted inside the frame), plaster walls, and a tile floor and bath add interest, while a neutral palette maintains calm.

Found treasures reused. An original sunken, tiled tub in this 1927 adobe-style cottage anchors the bath, and floor tiles, acquired from a European villa, accentuate the old-world feel. The salvaged antique farm sink is a find from Provence.

Gone-to-the-spa feel. The French soaps and organic sponges and brushes, all under the glow of an antique crystal-and-iron chandelier, project the spa-like vibe of a pampering retreat.

sink *(details)*

(The variety of sink designs has increased dramatically to accommodate the multifunctional purposes—from guest to master bath—and sizes—from expansive to closet dimensions—of modern bathrooms. Years ago, choosing a sink meant deciding between cast iron and porcelain. Today, the lingo you need to know can be a bit overwhelming. One option is the console sink, which works best in a clutter-free space where options for storage are independent of a typical vanity with cabinets. The sink is seamlessly incorporated into a vanity-style porcelain countertop supported by two legs. A basket underneath holds towels, and essentials are stowed away elsewhere, out of sight.)

(washstand)

(pedestal)

(bowl on top)

(under-mounted)

(built-ins)

(wall-mounted)

(**washstand**) First used in the 18th century, a washstand was a piece of furniture, usually found in the bedroom, that held a basin and other provisions necessary for bathing. In the modern bath, a washstand refers to a sink basin directly connected to plumbing and set into a countertop, usually marble or tile, that is supported by a frame made of chrome, nickel, or wood. The frame often provides a convenient place to hang towels.

(**pedestal**) Pedestal sinks, which come as one unit in all shapes and sizes, typically make good choices for small baths where little countertop or cabinet space is needed.

(**bowl on top**) This modern trend takes on the look of a bowl that appears to have been set down on the countertop. Keep in mind that faucets often need to be wall mounted, which requires a spout long enough to reach into the sink.

(**under-mounted**) Self-rimming sinks come in two varieties, under-mounted (shown here) and drop-in. Pay attention to the holes (typically one to three) provided for the faucet and knobs because they will determine the type of hardware needed. Some under-mounted sinks require that the hardware be set into the countertop, rather than fitted into cutouts in the sink.

(**built-ins**) A recent trend is to drop a sink into any old piece of furniture to create a unique, one-of-a-kind look.

(**wall-mounted**) Usually left with the plumbing exposed, the sinks shown here have cabinets underneath for a custom look.

fresh ideas: *bathroom extras*

Where function is always top of mind, pretty isn't always lost. These bathrooms show a flare for style that performs.

(Antiques and art find a place in the master bath.)

(Baskets, instead of drawers, hold necessities.)

(Decorative finishes make a big impact in small baths.)

(Two showerheads are better than one.)

(An oversize mirror provides an unexpected surprise in a bath with extra-tall ceilings.)

pulling it all together:

start with...

Bathtub. The average size of a bathtub is 30 by 60 inches. The drop-in model is usually sunk into a platform covered in wood or tiles, while corner units are attached to the wall.

Freestanding bathtubs work best as a focal point for a room; they come in a wide variety of styles, ranging from old-fashioned claw-foot tubs to modern styles, some of them made of copper.

It takes special hardware to incorporate a shower into a freestanding tub, so in a small bath with no separate shower, it's typically best to go with a drop-in model.

add...

Hardware. Keep the style of the sink, bathtub, and shower in mind when choosing the hardware, and remember that all of the hardware should be in the same finish (polished or brushed nickel, chrome, brass, or crystal). There is no standard size for faucets for freestanding tubs—just make sure the faucet is tall enough to direct water efficiently into the tub you choose.

Pay attention to the number of holes in a vanity sink to determine if two individual knobs and a separate faucet (three holes) are needed, or if the knobs and faucet should be purchased as a unit (one hole).

set up the...

Shower. There are two options for glass shower doors: framed and unframed. Framed doors, which are the most common, must be sealed when installed to avoid leaks. Unframed doors, which are made of heavier glass with less chance of leaking, have become the sleek choice for a modern look.

The classic shower curtain, either ready-made (the standard size is 70 inches by 72 inches) or custom-made, is still a good choice for meeting the style quotient in the bath.

accessorize with...

Towels, seating, and **extra storage.** Aside from necessity, towels are a simple way to add color.

If space allows, consider using a bench for storage; or add storage baskets.

home offices

As the appeal of working from home spreads, more and more Southerners are creating functioning—and, of course, stylish—home office spaces equipped with the latest technological and organizational tools. Some designate entire rooms for workspace, while others carve out an area of the living room or a bedroom to get the job done. And it's not unusual these days to see a dining room table do double duty as "command central" for both work and entertaining.

This trend is encouraging designers to offer more fashionable options, from modern takes on the traditional office chair to eclectic versions of the typical desk or task lamp—all in colors that pop like eye candy. Even the techno world has upped the style ante with sleek computers and accessories that complement the aesthetics of modern home interiors. Another day at the office has, perhaps, never been so stylish.

(Right) Floors painted black and white and a vintage Jacobsen Swan chair in green leather add graphic punches to designer Christy Ford's office, conveniently situated just off the dining area of her home in Charlottesville, Virginia. She placed an oversize mirror in the space to capitalize on the sunshine.

dynamic duo

Home office designed by Kim Zimmerman
Atlanta, Georgia

Why it works:

Mirror image. Symmetry rules in this office for two: a pair of windows along with a double set of drawers center the desktop, matching wall units provide storage on both sides, and a dual fixture casts light evenly to both the left and the right.

Color consistency. A crisp red-and-white color scheme is interrupted only by simple polished nickel cabinet hardware and the coordinating light fixture. "I think of it as 'jewelry' for the room," says designer Kim Zimmerman.

Revealed and concealed. The open shelving that keeps frequently used items on display balances the ample drawers and cabinets that provide hidden storage.

haute headquarters

A corner in designer Jenny Keenan's living room
Charleston, South Carolina

Why it works:

Fancy yet functional. Antique secretaries have gained the reputation of being nothing more than pretty family heirlooms, but they once functioned as the most common and efficient piece of office furniture. In fact, many of their amenities—pigeonholes for storage, extra drawer space, and a retractable desktop—still have a lot to offer.

Location, location, location. A silver julep cup and other classic regional treasures reveal the whereabouts of this home office tucked away in designer Jenny Keenan's living room in Charleston.

Sentimental significance. Many of the area's settlers came from Europe, bringing with them lots of furniture. "Rooms in Charleston have a collected look rich with layers of history," Keenan notes. "If you don't include traditional pieces, you're cheating all the people who lived in your home before you." The room's hand-painted wallpaper also honors a unique Charleston tradition. "Today's twist is to pick a classic pattern rendered in a fresh color," Keenan explains.

designer cue

Long before the techno boom, a "real" secretary would handle operations for an employer, and the secretary desk was essential. These desks characteristically had two sections, bottom drawers and top hutch, with a folding plank for writing, which works great for modern laptop computers. Expect to pay anywhere from $3,000 to upward of $30,000 for a secretary desk, depending on its pedigree.

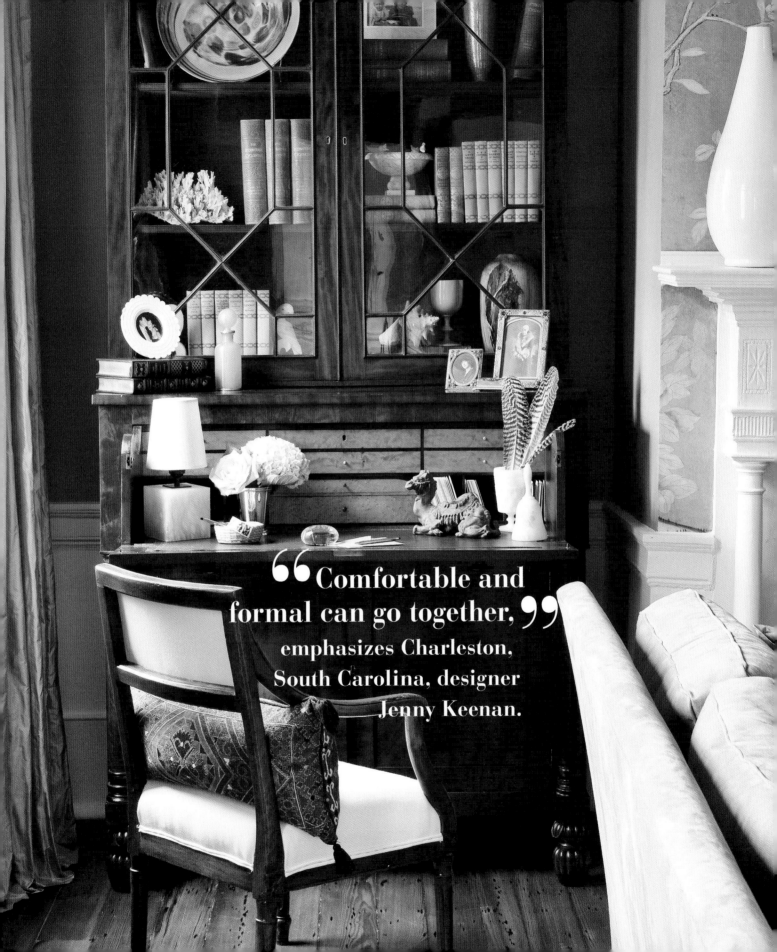

"Comfortable and formal can go together," emphasizes Charleston, South Carolina, designer Jenny Keenan.

repurposed retreat

Home office of designer Jennifer Hunter
Blue Mountain Beach, Florida

Why it works:

Smack-dab in the open. To eliminate minimally used rooms and wasted space, designer Jennifer Hunter chose to turn an unused third bedroom into a multiuse sitting room—a comfortable, functional retreat for reading or working.

Cheerful color. The incorporated workspace didn't slight the style factor. It features striking white walls offset with colorful, patterned Roman shades in place of art, plus a complementary green ceiling.

Mail order made easy. Many of the elements in this relaxed home office, including the Parsons-style desk with a washed wood finish, wall-mounted bookshelves in white lacquer, and the Louis Ghost Chair, are available through mail-order catalogs, as well as online.

he said/she said

Home office of architect David Colgan
and designer Tyler Colgan
Atlanta, Georgia

Why it works:

Hidden potential. Shutter doors, found
in a salvage shop and mounted on a track
slide, open to reveal the his-and-her office of
Atlanta architect David Colgan and designer
Tyler Colgan. The doors also serve an adjoin-
ing powder room.

1-2-3 access on the fly. With little children
in the house, the Colgans can't tuck themselves away in an obscure corner to work,
so they situated their shared work quarters
where the family is—the family room. This
makes it easy for them to seize snippets of
opportunity to send an email or jot down a
to-do list.

Cubby capacity. Cubbies take on a different
vibe than bookshelves—each space is its
own vignette. The Colgans stylized some
with art and pottery and stuffed others with
much-referenced books and magazines. The
randomness seems a bit less chaotic in here
than it would on traditional shelving.

fresh ideas: *creative office spaces*

No longer hidden away with a stodgy desk and swivel chair, home offices find themselves tucked into the most decorated spaces of the house, even sharing time with the dining room.

(This square table offers room enough for two. Opting for furniture with exposed legs leaves visible floorspace, a design trick that fools the eye, making rooms seem larger.)

(This dining room does double-duty as both a home office and a space for entertaining guests.)

(This sentimental piece, a dining table crafted by a favorite uncle in the 1930s, functions just as well as a desk.)

(With no room available elsewhere in the home, the owners put an office on the stair landing.)

pulling it all together:

start with a...

Desk. New styles of industrial tables look chic in spare spaces, but keep in mind the room where the table will be used.

If you're incorporating a desk into your living room, or if it happens to double as the dining room table, you might want to keep a more **traditional look.**

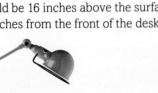

If you require more storage, it's a good idea to find a desk with **drawer space.**

add the...

Chair. Comfort is paramount, but remember style, too. New **modern shapes** pair well with traditional desks for an interesting contrast. Seating is available in a variety of patterns and colors, so it can function like an accessory in the room.

If you like the modern look but want extra comfort, try a **graphic shape** with a **padded seat.** Of course, a cushioned seat and back can be punched up with **fabric.** A little bit of frou-frou looks super-energetic alongside an industrial desk.

get bright ideas with...

Lamp. Decorative ones can do the job as long as they're tall enough. The light source should be 16 inches above the surface and 13 inches from the front of the desk.

Modern **task lighting** with adjustable height is the most flexible choice and looks surprisingly good in a traditional setting.

Some task lamps on the market don't have quite the **industrial look** but still offer the same advantages of direct, focused illumination.

finish the job with...

Technology and accessories. An assortment of cool accessories can add energy, which makes menial tasks like paying bills less boring.

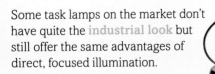

There's never been more to choose from in organizational **boxes** and **bins**, sleek **laptops**, and stylish **wastebaskets.**

The kids are really aware of their surroundings so our home is completely a family effort.
— Christy Ford

kids' rooms

Even in Southern homes that seem to be overflowing with children and their many things, there's style galore behind the apparent chaos. Believe it or not, children's domains are where many designers play up style to the max with vibrant colors, fanciful printed fabrics, and imaginative wall art.

For instance, designer Christy Ford decorated most of the rooms inside her Charlottesville, Virginia, house in a neutral palette layered with textures and understated pops of color. However, she took a more capricious approach in her daughters' rooms, where she painted the walls pastels and layered the beds with mismatched floral prints and polka dots. "The kids are really aware of their surroundings so our home is completely a family effort," she notes. She insists on letting her children explore the backyard for such things as feathers and birds' nests (abandoned, of course) to display on bookshelves and mantels. "Not only will they learn to love nature, but they'll also learn to respect the items displayed in our home," she explains.

Other designers are also taking unpredictable approaches in rooms for children and teens, like choosing a leopard carpet accented by a feminine pink fabric, a faux moose head instead of a piece of art, and tricked-out bunk beds for sleepovers as seen on the pages that follow.

165

sleepover heaven

Bedroom designed by Paige Lee
Grayton Beach, Florida

Why it works:

Custom cut. A design sketched on a piece of paper by the homeowner and handed to her builder became a permanent solution to accommodate her sons and their constant (and oh-so-welcome) houseguests.

Bold contrasts. Grayton Beach, Florida, designer Paige Lee chose rich royal blue walls to highlight the white beds, which she accented with mostly red quilts and pillows.

Heirlooms-made-mod. This room holds heirlooms the homeowner previously never had a spot to display, including her grandmother's old quilts and a footstool she brightened with paint.

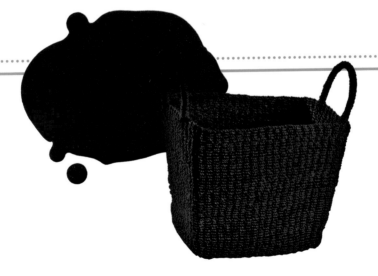

light *and* airy

Designed by jewelry and fabric designer Kitty White
Birmingham, Alabama

Why it works:

Texture to the max. Sheer curtains, a crusty wood console, and a plush shag rug add depth to this room. "I've realized that going to the extreme with one color is fun when you play up different textures," explains Birmingham jewelry and fabric designer Kitty White.

Plush comfort. The rug and bed linens soften the wood furnishings and create a comfortable retreat to curl up with a book. A loosely slipcovered chair plus the throw enhance the cozy appeal.

Not-too-little girlie. Sophisticated elements, like the framed botanicals and an antique tole chandelier, add a mature quality to what will become a preteen room before long.

function *and* style

Bedroom designed by Lee Kleinhelter
Atlanta, Georgia

Why it works:

Playful color and fabric. The geometric-patterned fabric and bold furniture in aqua, orange, and chocolate brown pop against the white walls, visually enlarging the small space. The tailored bed skirt and headboard in the same fabric stand out as a focal point. "I love this geometric print," says Atlanta designer Lee Kleinhelter. "You can make it feel youthful or more sophisticated depending on the accessories you use."

High performance. Fashionable color and fabric make this room practical for many uses. When it's not occupied by Kleinhelter's preteen, it sometimes functions as a guest room. It could also easily be transformed into a home office.

Smart storage. A bookshelf adds architectural interest to this room. Homemade tags, cut from plywood and painted with chalkboard paint, label the felt baskets in the cubbies to help keep toys and games organized. "The felt baskets are a modern take on traditional woven ones, and they've totally simplified our life," Kleinhelter notes.

> **My goal was to make this room useful and stylish.**
> — Lee Kleinhelter

designer cue

Daybeds provide a versatile option for smaller bedrooms that can't accommodate lots of furniture. Their multifunctions—sofa by day and bed by night—are particularly nice, especially if you don't have a designated playroom.

lad's pad

Boy's bedroom designed by Charlotte Moss, Tulsa, Oklahoma

Why it works:

Decorator details. The bells and whistles that designer Charlotte Moss uses are clearly evident in—yet subtly suited for—this little boy's room. She used an overall, subdued green palette to maintain restraint when selecting the multi-patterned custom-fabric lampshades, carpet, custom cornice, and cascading fringed curtains.

Sofa-bed combination. Positioned in a custom-designed niche, the daybed acts as sofa for reading books and watching movies with friends, as well as a bed when it's time for "lights out."

Room to grow. These highbrow furnishings will grow with the child, but for now they easily welcome all of the child's treasures, including a big stuffed frog and plastic truck. A woven basket successfully accommodates other playful companions.

wild at heart

Bedroom designed by Joanie Herring
Houston, Texas

Why it works:

Not too "theme-y." A fascination with wild animals inspired this boy's room—punchy accents and a fearsome stuffed lion grab attention and spark the imagination. It's smart to use relatively subtle themes, such as animals, nautical, or circus rather than superheroes, which kids tend to quickly outgrow.

Grown-up accents. The sophisticated framed prints and photographs are paired with fun stuff, like the inflatable deer's head and a Richard Scarry book that doubles as artwork. In addition, tailored, masculine fabrics complement child-friendly elements—figurines, favorite books, a tepee, and an activity table that encourage fantasy and fun.

Open shelving. Knowing where things go makes for quick and easy clean-up, which encourages youngsters to lend a hand. As the child grows, the books and animals can be replaced with collections, trophies, and framed photos.

designer cue

Take a look around your child's room. It's a place he can grow with if you are able to take away the accessories and decorative items and have a relatively blank slate to reinvent. Infuse the area with personal accessories, not necessarily a mural on the wall or layers of Mother Goose fabric framing windows and covering furniture. Children grow fast, so keep the space versatile.

girlie meets glam

Bedroom of writer Amy Bickers's daughter, Birmingham, Alabama

Why it works:

Expect the unexpected. A frilly bed in layers of pintucked white linen is accented with a ruffly trim, but it is offset by the bold bubble-gum walls. This strong pink color is tempered by lots of white accents.

High-fashion details. Cleverly framed pages from fashion prints set a haute couture tone, while a clear acrylic console serves as both desk and dressing table with a dash of glitz.

Pink, pink, pink. This color has many nuances—from ladylike to punk rock. Everything in this room has a hint of pink: from books, basket, and lampshade to the framed monogram prints above the tufted headboard covered in creamy shantung silk.

teen spirit

Teenage girl's bedroom designed by Mia James
Baton Rouge, Louisiana

Why it works:

Super-cool headboard. This one is made in two panels, with a frame that almost touches the ceiling. In fact, Baton Rouge, Louisiana, designer Mia James created it to match the height of the curtains, which are made of the same fabric, to make the small room appear bigger.

Art that rocks. Unframed and funky, this pair of elongated paintings, which feature birds on a perch, has a graphic appeal that teens love, as well as soft, pretty colors that make mom happy.

Hot color. James suggests finding a few colors that speak to you and sticking with them. Hits of aqua—the lampshade, paintings, headboard, and curtain fabric—add color to the neutral background. Monograms (which teens also love) give yet another subtle pop.

designer cue

Bring balance to space with color. The colorful print on the tall headboard is mirrored in the curtains across the room. The turquoise vignette on the dresser is balanced by the skirted table and accessories across the room.

fresh ideas: *kids' rooms accents*

The fun begins in the rooms where children play and rest. Today there are countless options to create spaces where there's room to grow.

(The simple addition of a row of hooks for pint-size coats and sweaters quickly converted this room, which was once a home office, into a combination mudroom-library.)

(Don't go for the same old, same old crib. This round one has a fresh look that shakes up the look of a typical nursery.)

(Kids need conversation areas, too. Try slip-covering an old pair of chairs in a playful way, or go all out with a coffee table and sofa.)

> **"My look is airy and serene with graphic surprises."**

take it from
Liz Hand Woods:

For her blended family, Birmingham, Alabama, designer Liz Hand Woods found room in the family's stylish cottage for six children—and she encouraged all of them to express their individual styles in choosing fabrics and accessories for their rooms. Here are some of her secrets to keep things playful yet elegant. **1.)** "The boys are into hunting so I let them have their ducks and deer heads." Camouflage duvet covers complete the look. **2.)** The oldest girls wanted something stylish so Hand Woods created the tented twin beds. U-shaped rods mounted to the ceiling over the low beds hold the fabric, which adds height to the room. **3.)** Hand Woods created the illusion of a four-poster bed with a canopy by framing this bed with panels hung from the ceiling. "Frances loves pink," she notes about her youngest daughter. "So I just went with it." **4.)** Alabama artist Lila Graves painted the sophisticated, but not-too-stuffy, children's portraits that hang in the playroom.

pulling it all together:

start with...

Creative furnishings. Though it's smart to choose pieces that can grow with your child through his or her teenage years and beyond, heirlooms are certainly not out of the question for play spaces—a child's room is still meant to be fun as well as functional.

Consider things that can adapt over time, like **a chest** with good storage— the wheels can easily be traded for legs.

Something vintage is great for conversation—a pair of **textile stools** can be used now as a perch for chatting with buddies and later as a footstool paired with a comfy wing chair.

add...

Whimsical lighting. Children need ample light for daily activities like reading, playing, and coloring. Plus, lighting provides another opportunity to amp up the fun factor.

Choose fixtures that have graphic appeal, accent colors, or **show-stopping charm.**

get organized with...

Functional shelving. Open shelving is easily visible and helpful for encouraging children to participate in cleaning up the room. **Baskets** are great for organizing items, like toys and games, and for keeping them out of sight.

accent with...

Colorful fabrics. Just a touch of color, with a favorite fabric on the seat of a chair or a funky pillow thrown on the bed, can differentiate children and teen spaces from adult rooms.

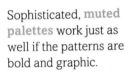

finish with...

A funky rug. Rugs provide softness for floor play and also help buffer the noise, not to mention adding another burst of color or pattern.

Sophisticated, **muted palettes** work just as well if the patterns are bold and graphic.

Consider durability and washability— **outdoor fabrics** work well in spaces that get a lot of wear and tear, especially benches, seats of chairs, and other favorite perches.

reinventing
the old

then *and* now

Gather inspiration from Southern tastemakers who have learned to adapt their furnishings (often simply by moving them from room to room) in fresh ways that accommodate their lifestyles and look super chic.

from Guest Room to Living Room

then!

(2005) Style Director Heather Chadduck inherited these circa 1979 cabbage-rose curtains and valances from her mother. "The minute I spied them, I knew I could update them," she recalls. Attached to the wall, instead of the window, they highlight the wicker headboards and make an instant statement. "Hang them as close to the ceiling as possible for a grand effect," suggests Chadduck. "Plus, your ceilings will look taller."

now!

The hand-me-down curtains have moved from the guest room to the den, where they remain open to let in natural light, adding a punch of color to the mix of neutrals and natural textures.

INTERIORS

from Orange to Yellow

then!

(2006) Atlanta designer Lee Kleinhelter spotted the modern wall canvas one day when she was shopping. "It was part of a store display," she explains. "When I saw it, I begged the owner to let me buy it." The pop art found its way into her home, where she paired it with a classic rattan reclining chair. "I try to mix old and new with an updated approach," she notes.

now!

In Pieces, her home furnishings shop, Kleinhelter is always transforming furniture with easy fixes like paint and upholstery, and her house mimics this approach. In her new home, she gave the wall canvas a fresh look with bright yellow paint. "I just got a brush and painted over it," she says unapologetically.

" I look at decorating from a standpoint of **what's going to come with me when I move again.** "

—Lee Kleinhelter

> 66 There's no law that says a dining room **has to be a dining room.** 99
> —Christy Ford

from Dining Room to Sitting Room

then! ·······································

(2005) When designer Christy Ford and her husband moved to Charlottesville, Virginia, from New York City, this 1911 cottage became their home. The gray walls of their formal dining room complemented a landscape painting by University of Virginia art professor Dean Dass. She found the 19th-century French server and pine Belgian farm table on buying trips for her antiques and accessories shop,

now!

Soon after the couple settled into their cottage, they started their family…so the dining room became a much-needed casual, comfortable family room with new furnishings and a warm shade of cocoa on the walls. Only the glam antique chandelier, which Ford discovered on a trip to Paris, remains from the original decor.

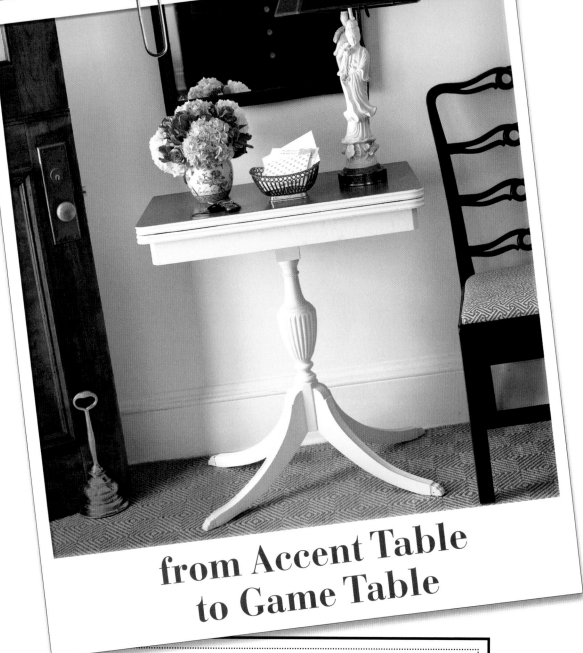

from Accent Table to Game Table

then!

(2011) Style expert and flea market fanatic Eddie Ross found this reproduction pedestal table at an antiques show. Painted white and accented with a deep pink top, it looks super chic in the entry—doubling as a catchall for keys and mail.

now!

Unfolded and painted with white stripes, Ross moved the table to the corner of a sunroom as a new spot for game night. A hidden drawer lined with pink scrapbook paper reveals cards, dice, and other accoutrements for friendly competition.

from Entryway Perch to Breakfast Table Seating

then!

(2006) Editor Beaty Coleman chose an easy-to-clean faux ostrich vinyl to give a modern look to an old settee. Placing it in the entry not only was pleasantly unpredictable, but it also made the tiny room multifunctional as both a mudroom for tying shoes or tossing everyday items and a conversation spot away from the children's television and toys.

note

In Coleman's new house, the settee gets a spot in the kitchen as seating at the breakfast table, where the color works perfectly in the all-white kitchen. "Lucky I had covered it in the vinyl—it's now our children's favorite seat in the house for most every meal," she notes.

from Traditional Style to Modern Flair

then!

(2006) Style Director Heather Chadduck's bedroom was cozy with a four-poster bed and humble, traditional fabrics—plaid, toile, burlap and a matelassé with a floral pattern.

now!

Maintaining a penchant for the coziness of four-posters, Chadduck updated her look with a newer, modern chrome version that she embellished with a floral-printed canopy to keep the cozy feel. She also upgraded her matelassé coverlet to work with the more streamlined look—this one has a simple diamond pattern.

three ways

Triple the potential of a single space or furnishing using these smart, stylish ideas from the experts.

(before)

Powder Room Transformation

a convenient Laundry Spot by day

A contractor built a platform to raise the washer and dryer for easy access. Beaded board lines the top half of the nook, and a concrete countertop provides a flat surface for folding laundry.

2 a Snazzy Bar at night

Two sconces and a mirror dress up the space and camouflage the laundry-room look, while the countertop conveniently serves as cocktail central. A pair of cafe curtains, crafted from a ready-made tablecloth, disguise the under-counter laundry space.

3 a Wrapping Station for the holidays

When holiday preparation is in high gear, the countertop transforms yet again with trays and baskets for paper, ribbon, and tags, making gift wrapping quick and easy.

(before)

Plain Door, No More

Groceries
Bottled H₂O
Paper towels
Wipes
Coffee
O.J.

1 Enhance usefulness with chalkboard paint.

Painting this door with chalkboard paint gives it both form and function as a convenient spot to jot down a grocery list and reminders as well as a surface for child-friendly wall art. The designer created the corners by tracing the edge of a saucer to add graphic appeal.

2

**Disguise the mundane
with a raised panel.**

While high-gloss paint gave this door a bit of
glamour, an attached panel—made from a piece
of plywood wrapped in batting foam, covered
in suede, and finished off with nailhead trim—
raised it to the next style level.

3

**Punctuate with a window and
upholstery details.**

After an 8-inch porthole window was punched
into this door, it went to an upholstery shop to be
covered in white, easy-to-wipe-clean faux vinyl
and decorated with a nailhead pattern.

A Trio of Chair Ideas

1 Choose leather for practicality.

"I love the idea of using patent leather on a classic chair to give it an edge," says Atlanta designer Betty Burgess. It's also practical for people who need something that cleans easily. The nailheads define the shape of the seat and give it a customized feel.

2

Go with a slipcover for an easy change.

Slipcovers are good for seasonal changes and can be dry cleaned when necessary. "I kept the skirt short enough to show off the legs," explains Burgess. Contrasting ties and other handsewn details add to the one-of-a-kind look.

3

Keep it traditional.

"The floral fabric and delicate gimp trim are classically Southern," Burgess adds. She suggests bumping the trim all the way to the edge and blending—rather than contrasting—it with the fabric.

Layered Options

1 Style with textures.

"Muted colors lend a bit of masculinity, but the inter-play of textures softens the look," notes Birmingham designer Liz Woods. Adding a bolster pillow marries the various shades of gray, but the organic pattern keeps it from looking too feminine. With blankets, sheets, and coverlets neatly tucked, there's no need for a skirt. "Tucking creates a clean, finished look—another way to emphasize the headboard," she explains. "You can completely change the look of a bed by adding or removing a skirt."

2 Throw in a bold pattern.

Departing from her preferred all-solid linen approach, here Woods goes for it with pattern. "I was drawn to this one because it's not too overwhelming," she says. Solid velvet accent pillows—persimmon and green—provide richness with a sense of depth. The basket-weave bed skirt works well with the botanical feel. "A skirt should always just graze the floor—never too long or too short."

3 Blanket it in white.

"When I am working with white, I tend to layer the shades to give it dimension," Woods explains. The rectangular shape of the lavender ikat pillow mimics the headboard, and the colorful pattern contrasts the all-white frilliness of everything else. "It's the exclamation point," she emphasizes. A Ghost Chair next to the open form of a pedestal table lends further airiness to this ethereal room.

Three Paint Recipes Transform a Table

1

Unexpected

Though painting a room orange may not come to mind right away, there are hints of the color in the painting, and it certainly commands attention on the wall. Consider lightening up the autumnal color with fresh accents of green—seat cushions on the rattan ottomans (great to pull out for extra seating) and a bowl of fresh apples. Glass lamps are airy touches that don't compete with the shades' striking monograms—which echo the bold wall color.

2 Dark

3 Subtle

In this scheme the chocolate brown wall color dramatically highlights the stylized accessories, starkly contrasted in white. Because dark walls can become black holes, the hanging plates and slipcovered ottomans add lightness and draw greater attention to the artwork.

Choosing a light color doesn't mean lack of visual impact; rather, pale colors often attract attention without demanding it. A less symmetrical arrangement of accessories gives the room a more lived-in look. The rattan ottomans, now slipcovered in green velvet, and the white chairs flanking the table are a complementary approach to accessorizing, rather than going for high drama.

fill *in the* blank

Apply these tasteful solutions to liven up any wallspace in your home.

Fill in the Blank with...
a Gallery Wall

1 Trace shapes for size.

>2 Tape them up for placement.

Lay out all of your framed art pieces on sheets of kraft paper, trace around each piece, and label each outline.

Cut out the outlines, and arrange them on the wall, using painter's tape to hold them in place. Group small, similar outlines together to make a greater impact.

3

Determine nail placement.

Once you have an arrangement you like, mark the spot on the kraft paper where the nail will go. Hammer in the nail, take down the paper, and hang the framed piece.

4

Done!

Your random collection of framed pieces will fill the wall with pleasing cohesiveness, and your advanced planning means fewer misplaced nail holes to patch.

More Ways to Get the Look...

1 Repeat a color.

A more modern interpretation of the gallery wall, this mix of collected pieces, children's artwork, and faux antlers keeps it simple with a singular color—pink—that runs throughout.

2 Give leftover wallpaper a second chance.

Add pizzazz with a roll of floral-patterned wallpaper cut into pieces and displayed in ready-made frames.

3

Tack it up.

Fill a large, open staircase wall with a group of unframed prints and photographs simply tacked at the four corners for a casual, yet eye-catching, gallery.

4

Think symmetry.

Hung in a uniform fashion, this series of botanicals, each sealed between two pieces of glass and bound with bookbinding tape, looks super-chic, merging traditional art with a modern arrangement.

Get the Look with...
family photos

1 Use a wall-hanging system.

A simple wall-hanging system, available through many mail-order catalogs, helps organize photos in showstopping fashion.

2 Lean it on a ledge.

A collection of photos rests atop a ledge fixed to the wall with large hooks. The matching frames and mats create a family gallery that can be easily rearranged and added to over time—with no nail holes to worry about.

3

Tuck extras behind frames.

Photos in store-bought frames hung in three vertical rows fill in the narrow space between two doorways in this small den. Loose snapshots stuck to the wall between the frames create a quirky, lived-in look.

4

Hang it on a hook.

Here, a series of old family photos was copied and mounted on heavy cardstock. Holes punched at the tops of the mounted photos allow them to hang in a grid pattern—some of them even form triptychs—on tiny hooks in this entry.

Fill in the Blank with...
an Etched Mirror

1 Create and apply a pattern. > **2** Cut out the design.

Choose a design—either stock, stencil, or custom. This custom one was enlarged to be more dramatic, and then enough copies were made to frame the mirror. Cover the entire surface of the mirror with adhesive vinyl paper. Smooth on slowly to avoid bubbles. Then tape the pattern into place.

Cut out the part of the design you want to be etched using a craft knife. Be sure to make precise cuts, pressing firmly so the knife cuts through both the pattern and the adhesive paper. You will not harm the mirror. When finished cutting, carefully remove the pattern, exposing part of the mirror.

3

Etch your design.

4

Done!

Wear latex gloves to apply a thick layer of etching cream over your stencil, covering all of the exposed mirror. Brush first with up-and-down strokes, then brush side to side. Allow the etching cream to remain on the mirror for at least 10 minutes. Take the mirror to the sink and wash under running water. Peel off the remaining adhesive paper. Clean the mirror with glass cleaner.

Prop the mirror on a buffet with a pretty tray, artwork, or other accents.

Fill in the Blank with...
a Custom Bulletin Board Calendar

1 . . . . >**2**

Evenly space ribbon vertically.

Evenly space ribbon horizontally.

Begin the grid with eight lengths of ribbon placed vertically. Use a sheet of paper as a spacing guide between the ribbons. Secure each end with an upholstery tack. Adjust the dimensions to the size of your wall, remembering to allow room at the top to display the months and days of the week.

Create six horizontal rows for your grid with seven lengths of ribbon, again securing each end with upholstery tacks.

3

Apply dates.

Adhere labels with self-fastening strips to make it easy to adjust the calendar monthly. The numbers and days of the week were created on a computer and printed on heavy cardstock. Use fonts and colors that complement your decor.

4

Done!

Fill your new, expansive wall calendar with invitations, reminder notes, and appointment cards—it's a great tool to keep a busy family organized and on time.

More Ways to Get the Look...

1 Catch-all in the kitchen

Divided into four distinct areas—a magnetic board for family photos, magnetic round containers for small storage, a corkboard for a calendar and invitations, and another magnetic board for children's artwork—boring kitchen cabinets transform into an attractive information station. Outlining the entire area with ribbon provides a unifying touch.

2 Reminders in a home office

Can't decide on a color? You can use them all by covering cork tiles (available at hobby stores) with squares of colored felt. Use a glue gun to attach the cut-to-fit squares onto a hollow-core door.

3

Revolving travel inspiration

Paint a basic bulletin board the same color as the wall, and use it to post dreamy vacation-scapes torn from magazines.

4

Organizer in the laundry room

It's not exactly a bulletin board, but it sure does the trick with a filing rack and magnetic board for posting invitations and pictures.

furniture
face-lifts

Reinvent your furnishings, whether tattered, heirloom, or even brand-new, with fabric, nailheads, paint, and these style secrets.

before: An estate-sale castoff

after:

A versatile, small-scale Chippendale-style settee, suitable for an entryway, breakfast table, or living room. Stripped down to its frame and re-upholstered in a favorite modern bird print, it reveals its traditional charm.

before: A tattered armchair

after:

A spot for reading that looks like a million bucks. Re-covered in a pretty botanical print and trimmed in a coordinating (but not matchy-matchy) linen and nailheads, this armchair is as good as new. Painting the legs white lightened the visual weight of the piece.

designer cue

If you are painting an upholstered piece—like this one that has a coat of off-white paint applied to the legs and arms—paint it before re-covering it. Lightly sand the wood first to help the paint stick. The "chipped" imperfections give this chair an appealing aged look.

before: An übertraditional antique

after:

A stylish and childproof dining chair—just wipe down the vinyl seats afterward. The faux-ostrich vinyl seats and backs and painted white frames take these dining chairs to a sleek new level, while monogrammed fabric backs add a personal touch.

before: A faux-gilded chair

after:

A stately piece painted to match the room's cream trim and re-upholstered (minus the tufting) in a graphite-toned mohair.

designer cue

Mohair adds a luxe touch that's worth the big bucks you can expect to pay for it. Taking the tufting out of old pieces (especially Victorian styles) when you re-upholster can instantly update the look.

before: A dust collector in the basement

after:

A showstopper re-covered in teal velvet. Here, selecting the right fabric is paramount. A light-colored solid with a little shine works best to define the clean, modern lines of this chair.

before: A stuffy Louis XVI-style chair

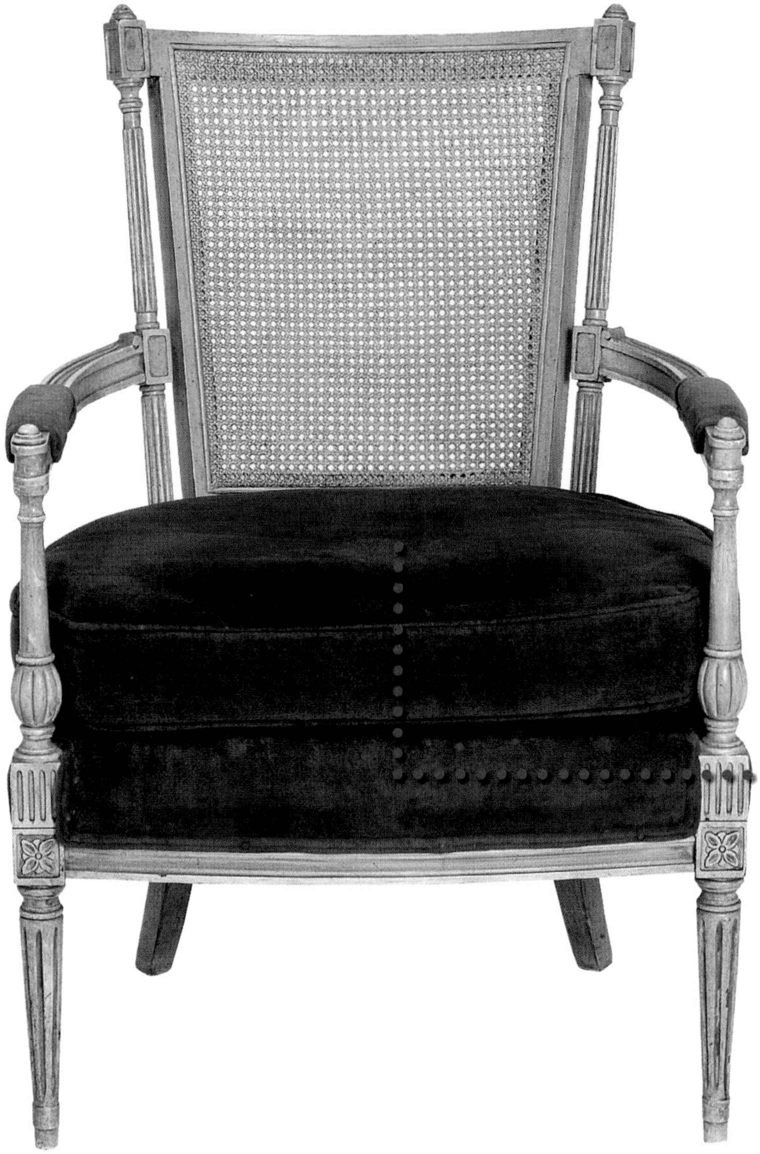

after:

A well-heeled French piece. Playful stripes lighten the look of this chair, while a cushy bolster pillow gives it a much-needed boost of comfort.

before: A dumpster-bound swivel stool

after:

A stylish place to sit at the bar, transformed with a coat of bright paint and a yard of textured (and durable) fabric on the seat.

before: An average cocktail table

after:

An ottoman in the dressing room. A seamstress topped the table with a 3-inch-thick piece of sturdy foam and then fashioned a box-pleated slipcover to fit snugly over both.

before: A $5-yard-sale sewing table

after:

A priceless sofa side table covered in wallpaper—a great option to revive furniture that's made of a lackluster wood. A wallpaper hanger gave this table a custom look by covering it with grass cloth and adding new hardware. If you're not practiced at working with wallpaper, don't try this yourself—hire a professional.

before: A "blah" wood console

after:

A swanky bar with a new coat of paint and a custom-cut limestone top. Any local kitchen or bath showroom can have a stone top cut to size for you—consider the same update for a coffee table or dresser top. For a smaller piece, like this one, scan the remnants section for bargains.

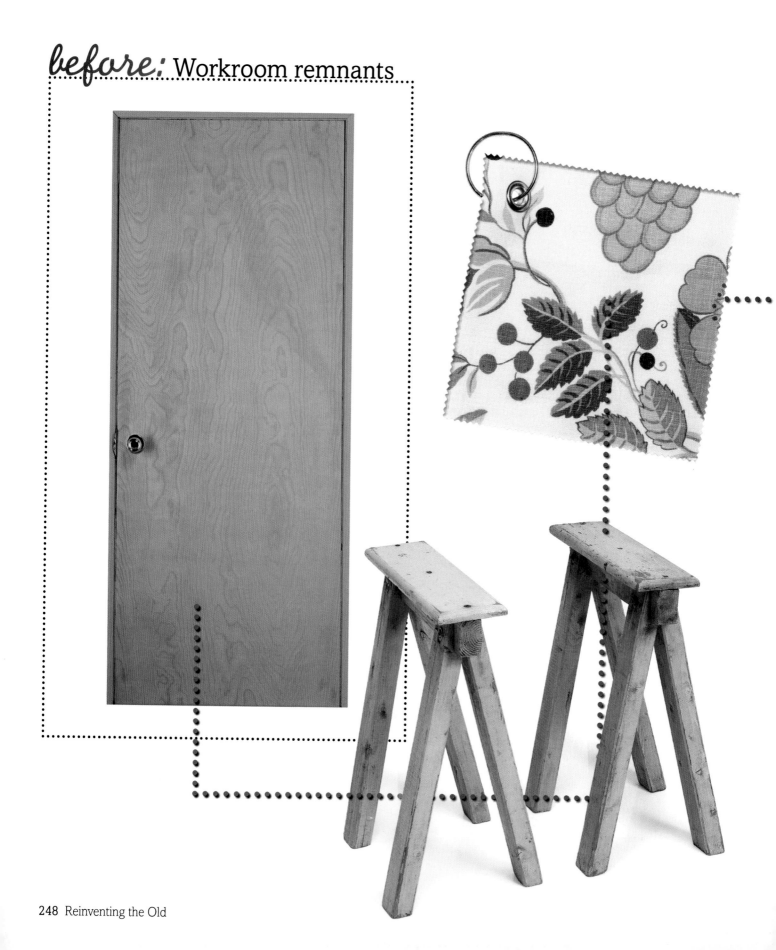

before: Workroom remnants

after:

A chic, functional desk made from a hollow-core door, two sawhorses, and leftover fabric scraps. Cover the door in a layer of felt before wrapping with fabric; the edges, finished with trim applied with nailheads, add oomph.

designer cue

If your desk isn't high enough, add casters to the sawhorse legs. To protect the fabric and provide a smooth writing surface, cover the desktop with a thin piece of glass.

before: A lucky yard-sale find

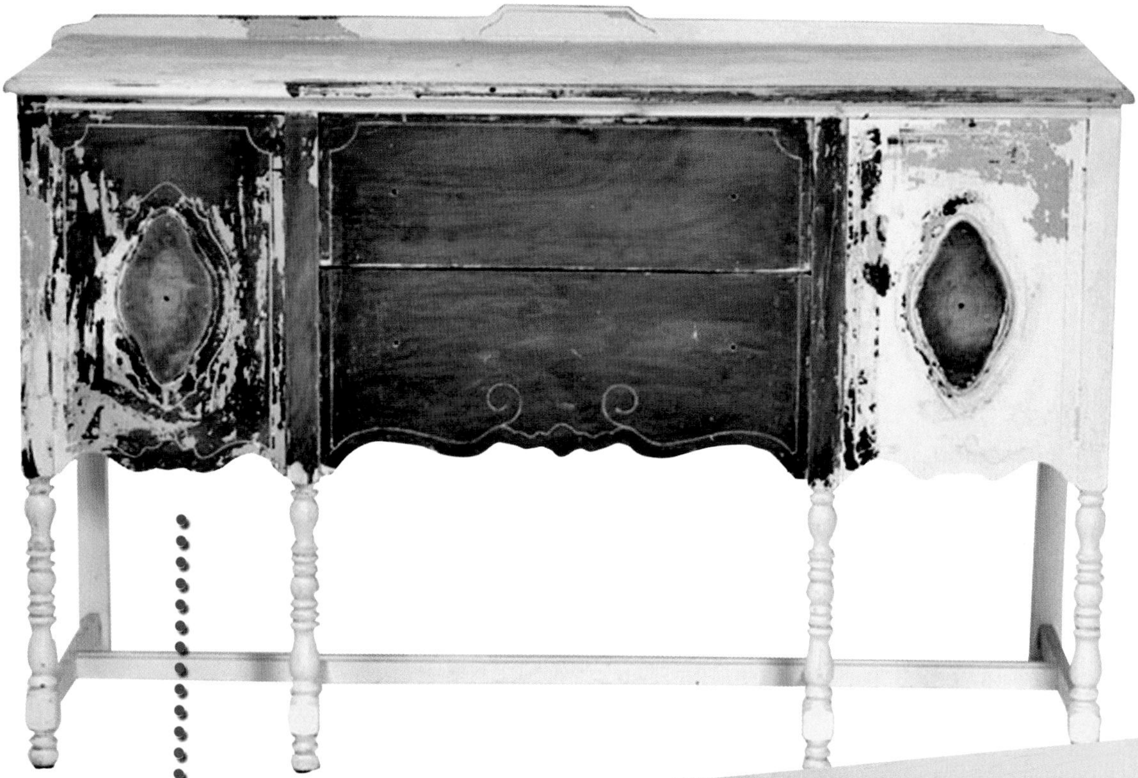

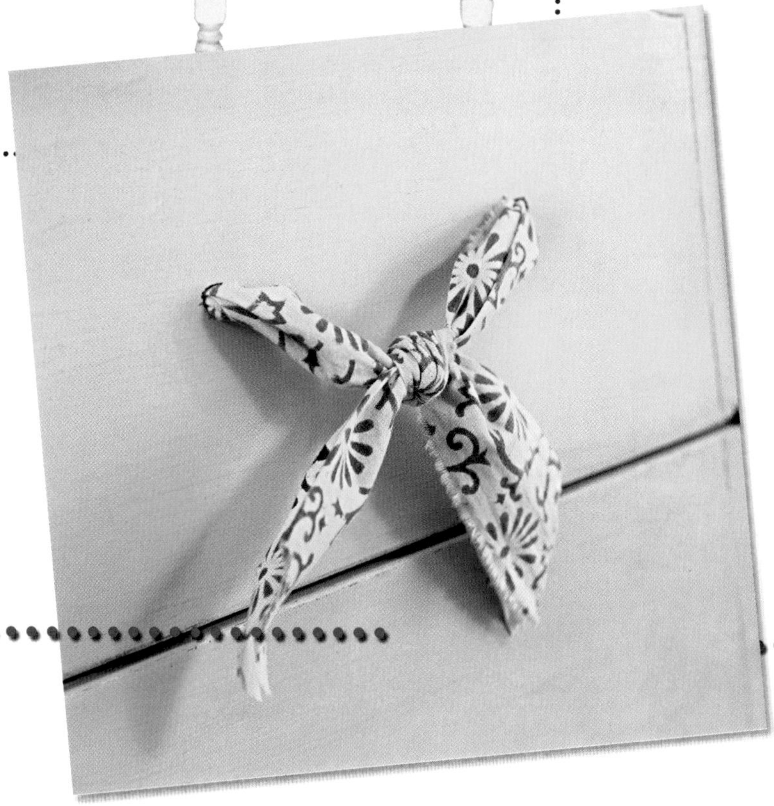

9/29 North Texas *
10/6 Tenn/Chat in LR
10/13 Auburn *
10/20 Ole Miss
0/27 FL Int'L *
1/3 South Carolina *
/10 Tennessee/Knox
11/17 Miss State in LR
11/24 LSU in Baton Rouge
* = Fayetteville

after:

A pretty storage piece with a fresh coat of paint. For a unique—and budget-friendly—flourish, the designer turned leftover scraps of fabric into clever drawer pulls that match a lampshade and pillow in the living area.

before: A ho-hum country console

designer cue

Opt for high-gloss paint when repainting furniture—it looks like a lacquer finish for a lot less money. In addition, you can cover a lot more surface with high gloss paints because coverage tends to be better, so usually only one coat is needed. Also, the higher the gloss, typically the more durable the paint, making it easier to clean the finished piece in the years of wear and tear to come.

after:

A stylish entry hall chest to hold odds and ends. High-gloss paint gives this piece a lacquered look that pairs well with the antique glass knobs.

before: A battered antique chest

after:

A shiny piece of art with potential to add interest in any room of the house. Sanded and repaired with wood filler, this chest gets glamorized with a metallic-accented wallpaper on the drawer fronts and matching paint. Glass knobs add sparkle.

before: A bachelor pad hand-me-down

after:

A pristine dresser with maximum drawer space that's too good to pass up. Consider giving it a coat of paint. Painting this piece the same color as the wall made it less noticeable and continued the light and airy feel of the room. If your walls are dark, the same concept applies—just use the same dark color.

before: A prefab cabinet

after

A new purchase that stylishly solves an obsession with shoes. This ordinary cabinet was brightened with pale blue paint, giving it a whole different look. Filled with shoe-storage cubes, along with plenty of space for boots and handbags, it's the most functional piece in the room.

before: A basic pine chest

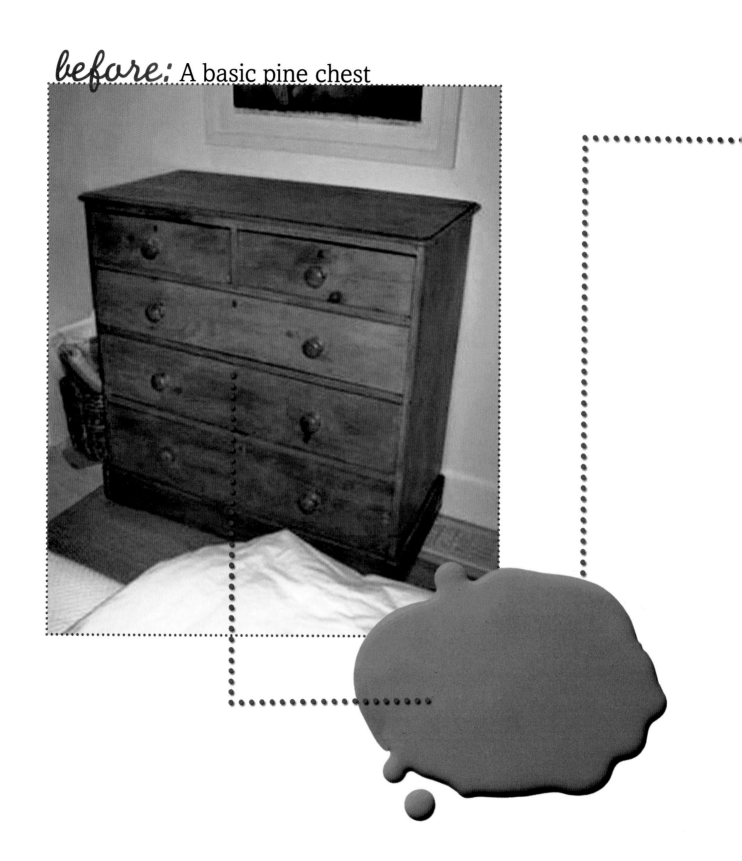

after:

A bright and cheery piece with a thick coat of high-gloss orange paint that elevates the mood. Instead of using new knobs, the original wooden ones get a coat of paint in a contrasting color, which adds a pleasing graphic touch.

before: A cherished antique bed

after.

A four-poster with personality—an antique-y feel with a modern look. The bold geometric pattern used for the canopy and bed skirt gives this heirloom piece an un-expected twist. Bordered in solid linen and pulled taut, the canopy appears to float atop the frame.

before: A utilitarian shelving unit

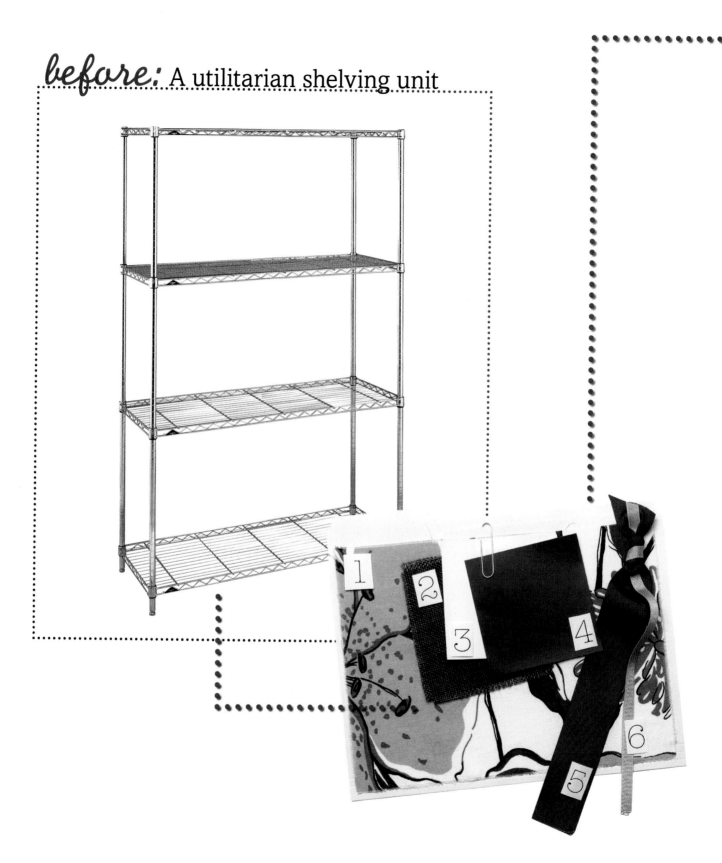

after:

An undercover home office with fabric panels
that open when it's time to work and close when
it's time to entertain. Most fabric stores can
recommend a seamstress in your area who can
make slip covering the shelving a cinch.

before: A mail-order folding screen

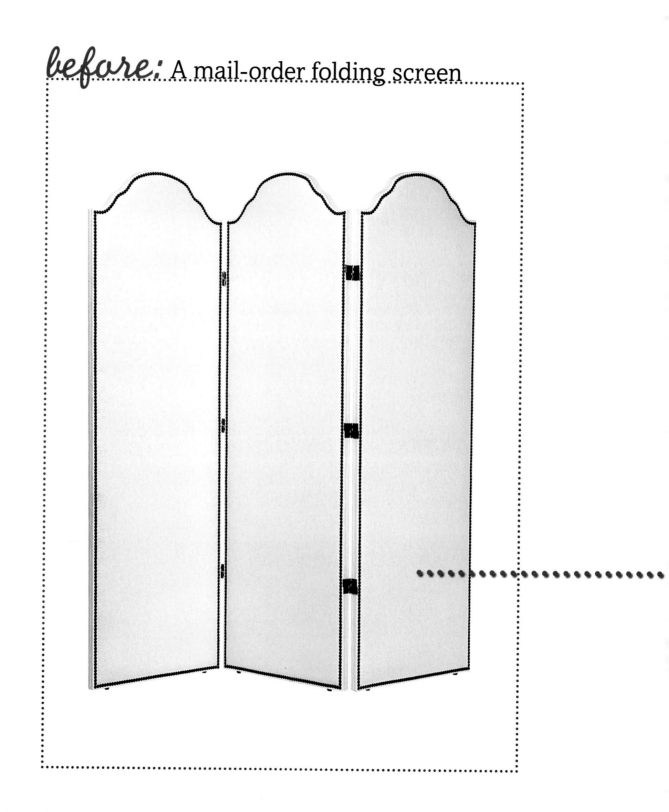

after:

A stylish headboard with a soft upholstered feel, perfect for comfort when reading and resting.

before: Salvaged fluted columns

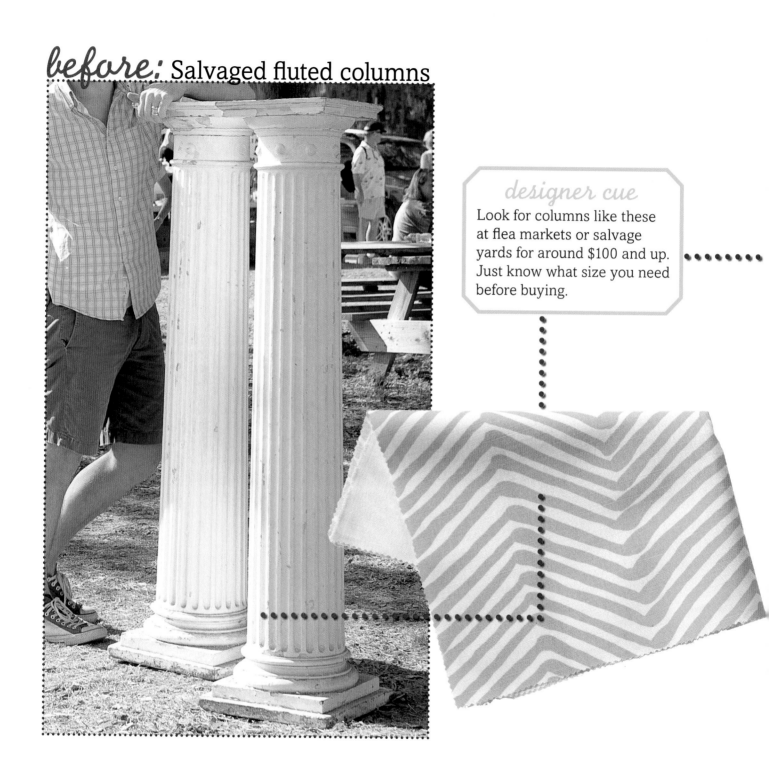

designer cue

Look for columns like these at flea markets or salvage yards for around $100 and up. Just know what size you need before buying.

after:

A punchy pair of floor lamps cleaned up with paint, wired for electricity using a standard lamp kit, and topped with drum shades wrapped in outdoor fabric, appropriate for the porch or even the living room.

southern style *file*

Room-by-Room Style Sheet

ENTRYWAY

Room measurements:

Window measurements:

Front door measurements:

brand:

style:

stain or paint color:

Walls

paint color:

wallpaper pattern:

Trim

paint color:

Window treatments

brand:

style:

pattern:

Flooring

type:

stain color or pattern:

Carpeting or rug

brand:

style:

pattern:

LIVING ROOM

Room measurements:

Window measurements:

Walls

paint color:

wallpaper pattern:

Trim

paint color:

Window treatments

brand:

style:

pattern:

Flooring

type:

stain color or pattern:

Carpeting or rug

brand:

style:

pattern:

KITCHEN

Room measurements: _____

Window measurements: _____

Walls

paint color: _____

wallpaper pattern: _____

Trim

paint color: _____

Window treatments

brand: _____

style: _____

pattern: _____

Cabinets and countertops

materials and brands: _____

_____

stain or paint color: _____

Flooring

type: _____

stain color or pattern: _____

DINING ROOM

Room measurements: _____

Window measurements: _____

Walls

paint color: _____

wallpaper pattern: _____

Trim

paint color: _____

Window treatments

brand: _____

style: _____

pattern: _____

Flooring

type: _____

stain color or pattern: _____

Carpeting or rug

brand: _____

style: _____

pattern: _____

BEDROOMS

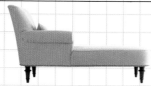

Room measurements: _____

Window measurements: _____

Walls

paint color: _____

wallpaper pattern: _____

Trim

paint color: _____

Window treatments

brand: _____

style: _____

pattern: _____

Flooring

type: _____

stain color or pattern: _____

Carpeting or rug

brand: _____

style: _____

pattern: _____

BATHROOMS

Room measurements: _____

Window measurements: _____

Walls

paint color: _____

wallpaper pattern: _____

Trim

paint color: _____

Window treatments

brand: _____

style: _____

pattern: _____

Tiles

style and brand: _____

_____

Fixtures

styles and brands: _____

_____

Flooring

type: _____

stain color or pattern: _____

HOME OFFICE

Room measurements: _____

Window measurements: _____

Walls

paint color: _____

wallpaper pattern: _____

Trim

paint color: _____

Window treatments

brand: _____

style: _____

pattern: _____

Flooring

type: _____

stain color or pattern: _____

Carpeting or rug

brand: _____

style: _____

pattern: _____

KIDS' ROOMS

Room measurements: _____

Window measurements: _____

Walls

paint color: _____

wallpaper pattern: _____

Trim

paint color: _____

Window treatments

brand: _____

style: _____

pattern: _____

Flooring

type: _____

stain color or pattern: _____

Carpeting or rug

brand: _____

style: _____

pattern: _____

Resources

Catalogs and Online Retailers

1stdibs.com
20x200.com
*Ballard Designs
Basicfrenchonline.com
*Beautifulpillowsandhome.com
Burkedecor.com
Conranusa.com
Countrydoor.com
Cspost.com
Curioussofa.com
*Dolcedimora.com
Echodesign.com
Etsy.com
FLOR
Garnet Hill
Gumps
Hayneedle.com
Highcamphome.com
*Highfashionhome.com
Home Decorators Collection
*Horchow
Laylagrayce.com
Lunabazaar.com
Onekingslane.com
Pearlriver.com
Plumparty.com
Quelobjet.com
Renovator's Supply
Rshcatalog.com
Serena & Lily
*Shades of Light
The Shade Store
Shopterrain.com

Smith + Noble
*Soft Surroundings
The Source Collection
Sturbridgeyankee.com
Sundance Catalog
Theelegantsetting.com
Threepotatofourshop.com
Tonichome.com
Topknobs.com
Velocityartanddesign.com
*Wisteria

Home Furnishings and Accessories

*Aidan Gray
*Antique Drapery Rod
Archatrive
*Arteriors Home
*Barbara Cosgrove
*Barn Light Electric
*Bernhardt
*Bevolo Gas and Electric Lights
Brahms Mount
Bungalow 5
Calico Corners
Campania International
Campo de' Fiori
Cath Kidston
Chelsea Textiles
*Circa Lighting
Comptoir de Famille
*C.R. Laine
*Currey & Company
Dash & Albert

*Drexel Heritage
*Elegant Earth
*Eloise Pickard Lighting
*Europe 2 You
*Gabby Home
*Global Views
Gray Line Linen
Hable Construction
*Hancock Fabrics
*Hickory Chair
*House Eclectic
Julian Chichester
Juliska
*LA Plates
*Lee Industries
*Leontine Linens
*Louisville Stoneware
*McCarty's Pottery
*Medina Baskets
Merida Meridian
*Mitchell Gold + Bob Williams
Mr. Brown Furniture
*Myers Carpet
Noir
*Orbix Hot Glass
*Peacock Alley
Pine Cone Hill
*Premier Prints
*R. Wood Studio Ceramics
Rejuvenation
Shine by S.H.O.
*Stray Dog Designs
*Tritter Feefer

*Vagabond Vintage through
   Mothology
*Vanguard Furniture
*Worlds Away
*denotes a company based in
the South

Our favorite stores across the South divided by region

Southeast

A. Tyner Antiques, Atlanta, GA,
   404/367-4484; swedishantiques.biz

And Beige, Washington, DC,
   202/234-1557; andbeige.com

And George, Charlottesville, VA,
   434/244-2800; andgeorge.com

Antiques on Holiday,
   Destin, FL, 850/837-0488

Bee, Atlanta, GA, 404/365-9858;
   bee-atlanta.com

Bungalow Classic, Atlanta, GA,
   404/351-9120; bungalowclassic.com

Circa, Charlottesville, VA,
   434/295-5760; circainc.com

Circa Interiors and Antiques,
   Charlotte, NC, 704/332-1668;
   circaonline.net

ESD, Charleston, SC, 843/225-6282;
   esdcharleston.com

The Farmer's Wife, Greensboro, NC,
   336/274-7920

Furbish Studio, Raleigh, NC,
   919/521-4981; furbishstudio.com

Gardenhouse, West Palm Beach, FL,
   561/832-8260;
   gardenhousedecor.net

Good Wood, Washington, DC,
   202/986-3640; goodwooddc.com

Interiors Marketplace,
   Charlotte, NC, 704/377-6226;
   interiorsmarketplace.com

John Pope Antiques,
   Charleston, SC, 843/793-4277;
   johnpopeantiques.com

La Bella Vie, Roswell, GA,
   770/645-1445

Lewis & Sheron Textiles, Atlanta,
   GA, 404/351-4833; lsfabrics.com

M Home & Garden & Interiors,
   Beaufort, SC, 843/524-7465;
   mhomeandgarden.com

Max and Company, Atlanta, GA,
   404/816-3831; Charlotte, NC,
   704/376-8050; Jacksonville, FL,
   904/384-6296; and Jacksonville
   Beach, FL, 904/241-4044;
   phoebehoward.net.

Mrs. Howard, Atlanta, GA,
   404/816-3830; Charlotte, NC,
   704/376-8900; Jacksonville, FL,
   904/387-1202; and Jacksonville
   Beach, FL 904/241-1980;
   phoebehoward.net.

No. Four Eleven,
   Savannah, GA, 912/443-0065;
   numberfoureleven.com

One Fish Two Fish,
   Savannah, GA, 912/447-4600;
   onefishstore.com

The Paris Market, Savannah, GA,
   912/232-1500; theparismarket.com

Pieces, Atlanta, GA, 404/869-2476;
   piecesinc.com

Pizitz Home & Cottage,
   Seaside, FL, 850/231-2240;
   theseasidestyle.com

Scott Antique Markets,
   Atlanta, GA, 404/361-2000;
   scottantiquemarket.com

ShopSCAD,
   Savannah, GA, 912/525-5180;
   shopSCADonline.com

South of Market, Atlanta, GA,
   404/995-9399; Charleston, SC,
   843/723-1114; southofmarket.biz

Star Provisions, Atlanta, GA,
   404/365-0410; starprovisions.com

Summerhouse,
   Greensboro, NC, 336/275-9655;
   summerhousestore.com

Tracery Interiors, Rosemary Beach,
   FL, 850/231-6755;
   traceryinteriors.com

Tucker Payne Antiques,
   Charleston, SC, 843/577-8515;
   tuckerpayneantiques.com

Vieuxtemps, Charleston, SC,
   843/723-7309; vieuxtemps.net

Southcentral

45 Flea Market & Antiques, Marion,
   MS, 601/679-7777

Ann Greely Interiors and Antiques,
   Lexington, KY, 859/367-0200;
   anngreelyinteriors.com

Antiques Within & Abbey's Too,
   Memphis, TN, 901/766-9044;
   antiqueswithin.com

Bittners, Louisville, KY,
   502/584-6349; bittners.com

Circa Interiors and Antiques,
  Birmingham, AL, 205/868-9199;
  circaonline.net
Gilchrist & Gilchrist,
  Nashville, TN, 615/385-2122
Henhouse Antiques,
  Birmingham, AL, 205/918-0505;
  shophenhouseantiques.com
Hudson Home,
  Louisville, KY, 502/384-4977;
  hudsonhomeliving.com
The Mustard Seed Emporium,
  Oxford, MS, 662/281-8004
Palladio Antiques & Art,
  Memphis, TN, 901/276-3808;
  palladioantiques.com
The Potager,
  Northport, AL, 205/752-4761;
  thepotagerofnorthport.com
Revival Uncommon Goods,
  Chattanooga, TN, 423/265-2656;
  revivaluncommongoods.com
Serenite Maison, Leipers Fork, TN,
  615/599-2071; serenitemaison.com
Sophie's, Chattanooga, TN,
  423/756-8711; sophiesshoppe.com
Southern Accents,
  Cullman, AL, 877/737-0554;
  antiques-architectural.com
South Front Antiques,
  Memphis, TN, 901/229-0299;
  southfrontantiques.com
Tracery Interiors, Birmingham, AL,
  205/414-6026; traceryinteriors.com
Tricia's Treasures, Birmingham, AL,
  205/871-9779; triciastreasures.us

Southwest

Bear Hill Interiors,
  Little Rock, AR, 501/907-9272;
  bearhillinteriors.com
Blue Print, Dallas, TX, 214/954-9511;
  blueprintstore.com
Brown, Houston, TX, 713/522-2151;
  shopbybrown.com
Ceylon et Cie, Dallas, TX,
  214/742-7632; ceylonetcie.com
Charles Faudree, Tulsa, OK,
  918/747-9706; charlesfaudree.com
Christopher Filley Antiques,
  Kansas City, MO, 816/668-9974
Cobblestone & Vine,
  Little Rock, AR, 501/664-4249;
  cobblestoneandvine.com
George, Kansas City, MO,
  816/361-2128; georgelifestyle.com
Indulge Maison Décor,
  Houston, TX, 713/888-0181;
  indulgedecor.com
Installations Antiques,
  Houston, TX, 713/864-6125;
  installationsantiques.com
Kay O'Toole Antiques and
  Eccentricities,
  Houston, TX, 713/523-1921;
  kayotooleantiques.com
Kuhl-Linscomb, Houston, TX,
  713/526-6000; kuhl-linscomb.com
Leftovers, Brenham, TX,
  979/830-8496; leftoversantiques.net
Lucullus, New Orleans, LA,
  504/528-9620; Breaux Bridge, LA,
  337/332-2625; lucullusantiques.com

Mecox Gardens, Dallas, TX,
  214/580-3800; mecoxgardens.com
Perch, New Orleans, LA,
  504/899-2122; perch-home.com
Pied Nu,
  New Orleans, LA, 504/899-4118;
  piednuneworleans.com
R. Ege Antiques, St. Louis, MO,
  314/773-8500; regeantiques.com
Shabby Slips Houston,
  Houston, TX, 713/630-0066;
  shabbyslipshouston.com
Somewhere in Time Antiques,
  Cape Girardeau, MO;
  573/335-9995
SR Hughes, Tulsa, OK,
  918/742-5515; srhughes.com
Uncommon Objects,
  Austin, TX, 512/442-4000;
  uncommonobjects.com
Urban Dwellings Design,
  Kansas City, MO, 816/569-4313;
  urbandwellingsdesign.com

Index

photography

ISBN-13: 978-0-8487-3470-1
ISBN-10: 0-8487-3470-X
Library of Congress Control Number: 2011933117

Printed in the United States of America
First Printing 2011

Oxmoor House
VP, Publishing Director: Jim Childs
Editorial Director: Susan Payne Dobbs
Senior Brand Manager: Daniel Fagan
Senior Editor: Rebecca Brennan
Managing Editor: Laurie S. Herr

Southern Living **Style**
Editor: Katherine Cobbs
Project Editor: Emily Chappell
Senior Designer: Melissa Clark
Production Manager: Theresa Beste-Farley

Contributors
Writer: Beaty Coleman
Designer: Blair Gillespie
Copy Editors: Norma Butterworth-McKittrick, Adrienne Davis
Proofreaders: Rebecca Benton, Dawn Cannon
Indexer: Nanette Cardon
Interns: Erin Bishop, Alison Loughman, Caitlin Watzke
Photographer: Mary Britton Senseney

Time Home Entertainment Inc.
Publisher: Richard Fraiman
Vice-President, Strategy & Business Development: Steven Sandonato
Executive Director, Marketing Services: Carol Pittard
Executive Director, Retail & Special Sales: Tom Mifsud
Director, New Product Development: Peter Harper
Director, Bookazine Development & Marketing: Laura Adam
Assistant Director, Brand Marketing: Joy Butts
Associate Counsel: Helen Wan

Southern Living
Editor: M. Lindsay Bierman
Creative Director: Felicity Keane
Managing Editor: Candace Higginbotham
Executive Editors: Rachel Hardage, Jessica S. Thuston

Homes Editor: Jennifer Kopf
Decorating Editor: Lindsey Ellis Beatty
Director, Editorial Licensing: Katie Terrell Morrow
Assistant Homes Editor: Zoë Gowen
Editorial Assistant: Marian Cooper

Directors of Photography: Julie Claire, Mark Sandlin
Photo Editor: Jeanne Dozier Clayton
Senior Photographers: Ralph Anderson, Gary Clark, Jennifer Davick, Art Meripol
Photographers: Robbie Caponetto, Laurey W. Glenn
Photo Coordinator: Megan McSwain
Photo Traffic Coordinator: Lee Anne Williams
Photography Department Assistant: Kate Phillips
Photo Archivist: Amanda Leigh Abbett
Photo Research Coordinator: Ginny P. Allen
Senior Photo Stylist: Buffy Hargett
Assistant Photo Stylist: Amy Burke
Studio Assistant: Caroline Murphy

Art Director: Chris Hoke
Associate Art Director: Erynn Hedrick Hassinger
Designer: Richie Swann
Art Assistant: Betsy McCallen

Copy Chief: Susan Emack Alison
Assistant Copy Chief: Katie Bowlby
Senior Copy Editor: Libby Monteith Minor
Copy Editor: Ashley Leath
Assistant Copy Editor: Jessica Stringer

Production Manager: Mary Elizabeth McGinn
Assistant Production Manager: Christy Coleman
Production Coordinator: Paula Dennis
Production Assistant: Ashley Riddle

To order additional publications, call 1-800-765-6400 or 1-800-491-0551.

For more books to enrich your life, visit **oxmoorhouse.com**